"I would like to congratulate Camille on writing this wonderful book highlighting her journey with eczema. Camille has written a very personal account and provides a number of techniques that can help to improve overall wellbeing. Eczema affects 1 in 5 people in the UK and it causes significant emotional and psychological upset. We currently have no cure for eczema. However, over 70 new medical treatments are currently being studied and we appear to be getting closer with some very exciting new biologic therapies. Camille's strategies for coping with and managing her eczema may help to reduce the severity of this condition."

Dr Tim Clayton,
Consultant Dermatologist,
Manchester, UK

how using the HOPE principles has changed lives

"My skin is now eczema free, my confidence has increased dramatically and I will happily leave the house with no make-up. Through gaining this confidence I have secured a promotion at work. You have changed my life." **- Hannah**

"Camille guided me when I was at one of my lowest points in life, helping me with my eating habits and, most importantly, supporting me when I didn't have anyone else. She is super patient and has always been there. I learnt I must nourish myself in and out." **- Bettina**

"I contacted Camille when I was feeling very low. I can't thank her enough for all the advice, knowledge, messages, love and healing power she has given me. Help, advice and support was only an email away. She gave me hope that I was on the right track and that I would heal. I feel like I have made a friend for life." **- Alice**

"I have Camille to thank for introducing me to a completely new way of living that's improved my health and my life no end. Camille is such a wonderful, positive and helpful person, she inspires me to keep learning. I know anyone would benefit and feel happier with a little Camille in their life." **- Georgia**

"I was going through a divorce, working hard and I have two small babies. I felt really low, had rashes up the side of my arms and my skin was dull and dry. Camille gave me advice on what to cook, prepare and buy when I went to the supermarket. Camille would always be there to help me and guide me in the right direction." **- Hollie**

"Camille changed my life. She helped me quickly understand the food and drink that made me wake up feeling horrible and helped me get my condition under control – so, even if I did have a flare up, I didn't worry. Thank you so much." **- Holly**

"Working with Camille has been the most amazing journey. She has helped me to improve my sleeping, eating and enjoyment of life. My physical appearance has improved as well as my thyroid condition, with bloating and digestion no longer troubling me." **– Kelly**

"My son has suffered from eczema since being a baby and was still suffering at the age of nine. Camille understood everything and was brilliant at giving advice on his diet and creams to use. She is professional in every way. Just a few little lifestyle changes has made a huge difference." **- Simone**

"After suffering with chronic eczema all over my body, but in particular my face, I began to develop severe social anxiety and a lack of confidence. I contacted Camille as I had tried every medicine and cream available to me. Camille's incredible knowledge and empathy, as a fellow eczema sufferer, helped me understand how important it is to own and love your imperfections. I am now 6 months completely eczema free and know that I am in control of my body. I can tell the signs of a flare up and can call upon all of the valuable lessons that Camille has taught me to ensure that the eczema stays to a minimum. I can't express my gratitude enough." **- Brogan**

"Camille has a positive energy, which, in itself is infectious and has taught me a whole new way of life; from cutting out unnecessary foods to people. Most importantly, I am now equipped with the tools and self-love I need to heal. The advice I have been gifted with is truly invaluable and I cannot thank Camille enough for her kindness whilst I am on my healing journey. I would encourage anyone to reach out to Camille!" **– Alex**

Contents

Introduction

Hello, beautiful person reading this.

You are not alone. We're in this together.

If you are one of the 330 million people worldwide who suffer from eczema, this book is for you. I've written the book I dreamt of finding five years ago to provide eczema sufferers with hope, understanding and support, and to equip people in the same situation as me with a life-changing toolkit.

When my skin got to a point where my whole body was covered in blood one morning after scratching, and the pain was unbearable, where I couldn't understand what was happening to me and the only support I could find online were of other sufferers complaining about their skin condition, I made a promise to myself to find a way out. I promised that once I'd found the answers, I would write a book to share my story and findings to give hope to every single person out there.

This is that book.

My emotional journey from rock bottom to optimum health took years of trial and error using natural therapies and medical intervention. Believe me, I have tried it all.

Over the following pages I share the ups and downs of that journey and reveal, for the first time, the methods I've used to heal myself from a condition doctors told me I would never recover from.

When your skin is in a terrible state, I know from experience, it makes life so much harder to handle and can start you off on a downward spiral which, unfortunately, only serves to make your eczema even worse. Add to that the sheer frustration of hearing from doctors that your eczema is in your genes and cannot be cured, and you're left feeling hopeless rather than hopeful.

have hope

Well, I'm here to tell you that there is HOPE. And that's why I've created the HOPE Principles, a framework for healing. Broken down into three core parts to share my story, explore stressors and support options, and provide a solid toolkit for managing the condition, *The Beauty of Eczema* provides an early warning system for how to manage eczema and thrive in life.

As well as the usual skin and diet recommendations which all books on the subject contain, I wanted to go one step further by shifting focus to the power of the mind and how mastering the mind can have a significant impact on reducing symptoms and getting in control of the condition. That's why this book explores stress as a cause, support as a strategy and the acronym HOPE as a set of guiding principles to help you go from victim to victor in an ultimate guide to coping with the condition.

The HOPE Principles provide you with a framework for healing, and I've been sure to combine scientific research and relatable anecdotes with a set of principles I now live my life by. The little life lessons will gently guide you towards a range of solutions that will help you, not only to manage your skin condition, but to flourish from this moment onwards.

I found out the hard way that just juicing wasn't going to fix skin ailments. Just exercising wouldn't either, and nor would just applying creams. So much more needs to be taken into consideration, from your home environment to your mental environment, from your level of optimism and your purpose in life to your self-care, exercise, food and how much time you spend outdoors. These are the seeds to plant and water in order to heal yourself of eczema and thrive.

The bottom line? If you want to manage and minimise your eczema, it's important to look at the bigger picture.

Imagine that big picture is a photograph of your future self, beaming with good health. Now imagine that image broken up into jigsaw pieces. You need each one to fit into place in order to create that picture of health. If one of them is missing, the picture of health is incomplete. It took me a long time to find every jigsaw puzzle piece, and here, across these pages, I share each of them with you, along with the story of how I found each one – from deep and painful sadness and raw anger to glimmers of gratitude and hope, joy and serenity.

I believe a positive mindset in life is key. Change is inevitable and life likes to test us all. But if we choose to move forward despite what tries to knock us down, that is where true courage lies.

As soon as I shifted how I saw my eczema to being a platform rather than a prison – a platform for helping me live my best life, rather than as something that would prevent me from doing so – I began to gain control over my skin and my life. And now you can do the same; now you can do as I have done and live a life feeling full of energy, with clear skin and a healthy mind so you can get on with living the life you've always dreamed of.

"Have the courage to follow your heart and intuition, they somehow already know what you truly want to become."
Steve Jobs

why this book is needed

According to the British Skin Foundation, sixty percent of British people currently suffer from or have suffered with a skin disease at some point during their lifetime, with 23 per cent of them suffering from eczema. The disease is more prevalent in children, with one in five having eczema. That's approximately 1.7 million school children in the UK alone.

According to the Health and Social Care Information Centre, in 2015, GPs in England wrote 27 million prescriptions for the topical agents used in the treatment of atopic dermatitis (eczema) at a cost of approximately £169 million.

That's why I believe that this book, which reveals from experience how to manage and minimise eczema, is so important.

What's more, there are also social and emotional implications that come with this physical condition. With eczema being apparent in the most visible places for adults (52% of us have our head and neck affected, and 50% our hands), it can adversely affect our self-confidence and cause social isolation. It certainly did for me.

Itching can be severe enough to interfere with sleep, causing tiredness and inability to concentrate at school and work. And, given the importance of sleep to physical and mental health, it's become even more essential to equip eczema sufferers with methods to manage their condition. Especially given that some reports suggest that eczema is on the rise.

how is eczema beautiful?

It may sound crazy to those of us who have been driven to the depths of despair because of our eczema. How can this frustrating skin condition be beautiful?

Well, I now truly believe, having eczema can be viewed as a blessing.

It forces you into living a healthier lifestyle, to listen to your inner child and listen to what he/she needs to thrive.

My eczema struggle helped me learn how powerful my mind is; it helped me listen to my body, to figure out which foods I thrive on, which positive thoughts are the most powerful in shifting how

I feel, and that stress can be soothed with the right self-care and external support. It's made me realise how strong I am. Now I want to show you how eczema can help you realise all those things too.

That's why it is called *The Beauty Of Eczema.*

Ultimately, I'm so thankful for what I've been through, despite being hospitalised and traumatised by how bad my skin got. Knowing that I have proved that you can gain control over your skin, no matter how bad it gets, is empowering.

Without having eczema and being driven to gain control over it, I would never have discovered these amazing life principles and tools which have hugely boosted my own wellbeing. Eczema led me here. Yes, having eczema has given me the opportunity to listen to my body. Eczema was, and still is, my signal that something isn't quite right. How useful it is to have this signal flagging up when I need to top up whatever is missing from my life; whatever is missing from my bigger picture of health!

That gift of knowledge is the beauty of eczema, my friends – an in-built signal guiding you towards a better life and a better you.

Consider this book a gentle hug from a friend who has been there, done that, made the mistakes and learned the lessons... and then risen and overcome the biggest obstacle of her life.

Love & Light,

Camille x

Part 1: Butterfly

"You will only see the brightest light when you have swum in the darkest water."

UNKNOWN

CHAPTER 1

Caterpillar

My head swam with fear as I leaned back on the hospital bed. The bright artificial lights above shone down on me, highlighting my feelings of anxiety and shame, magnifying them. What was going on? Just one year ago life was amazing. I'd been studying abroad and living the dream in California, skipping through life with clear skin, a blissfully good mood and a healthy body – and here I was sat in a hospital bed in intense pain with my head swollen to the size of a football, my skin raw and bleeding.

I'd recently moved away from my family again, this time from Lancashire to Swindon, to live with my sister and her friend. My dream internship had gone pear-shaped as a result of my condition and, for the past five months, I'd been suffering with the most severe case of eczema I'd ever experienced. It was covering my whole body, getting on top of me and pushing me down into the depths of despair.

Earlier that night I'd been feeling so low, I'd begun to lose hope. I felt like I didn't want to be here anymore. I couldn't live the rest of my life like this. I had Googled people with eczema, desperately trying to find stories of successful recovery, but all I found was one depressing forum after another depressing forum and a whole barrage of awful experiences – nothing positive at all. I couldn't bear to look at the screen of doom blinking in front of me, so I sank into my bed and cried.

I'd been putting bedtime off, because I knew I'd only end up scratching my body and making it even more raw. I was still bleeding from the night before. I'd had hardly any sleep for the past few months, and each morning I'd wake to find my sheets covered in dead skin and blood.

So I sat on my bed feeling more alone than I've ever felt. Isolated and dead inside, living a waking nightmare, and wishing I could fall asleep and wake up a year ago in California. I remember telling my friends over there how I 'used to' have eczema in England, as if I had conquered and cured it. Because, after six months in the sunny climate, I really felt that I had. As a result, I was too humiliated to speak to any friends. I didn't want anyone to know this was happening to me. I didn't even want to tell my dad. "What an embarrassment I am after losing my internship," I thought. "Such a liability!"

That cold gloomy night, as the bitter wind howled outside, I prayed this was all a bad dream, that this wasn't my reality.

But here I was, hitting rock bottom.

Life couldn't possibly get any worse than this.

All of a sudden, I felt a rush of heat rise up my body from my toes to my head. Over the next few minutes the hot sweats grew hotter and hotter until I looked in the mirror and noticed my face was swelling. I felt dizzy and the pressure on my head was unbearable. Being on my own, I began to panic. The throbbing was so intense at one point, I thought I might be dying.

Terrified, I grabbed my phone and called the only person I knew in the area: my manager, Kris. My sister and her friend were away at a party in London. My boyfriend back then was partying with his university friends in Cheltenham and my parents were back home up north.

It was late, but I told him I didn't think I could drive. "I'm seriously unwell," I told him. "The swelling is hurting and the pressure is getting worse, and I..."

"I'll be right over," he said calmly.

Kris had been my manager when I took an internship at a major health company and had taken me under his wing. He knew I was struggling with this condition, and had seen me transform from when I first joined the company looking reasonably well to becoming suddenly covered in eczema. Over the past few months, the eczema had worsened, but even he was shocked to see what had happened to me on this cold January night.

"Let's get you straight to A&E."

At the hospital, we sat quietly in the waiting room for a long time. I tried to avoid looking in the mirror on the wall. I could hear the phone ringing, machines beeping and hushed voices talking. The sound of footsteps echoed on the shiny vast corridors and were interrupted by the sound of my own thoughts.

"What on earth is going on?" I wondered. Everyone else, all the people I loved, were out there enjoying life, and here I was, a mess, sitting in a hospital waiting room with a work colleague rather than a loved one.

I was so grateful to my manager for going the extra mile for me. He didn't have to do this, so I deeply appreciated that he cared enough to help me when I needed it the most. Yet being with someone from work, instead of family or close friends, amplified my loneliness.

He was trying to make me laugh, but I just felt guilty to be wasting his time. He could be out enjoying his evening instead of sitting here with me in this cold and gloomy waiting room.

And besides, I was so far down in the depths of despair, my mind was focusing on all the negatives, rather than how good it was to at least have someone here with me and how kind he had been to help. Instead, I continued to think about how different life was now compared to my time abroad.

"Camille Knowles?"

Hearing my name pulled me back from my downward spiral and the doctor led me into a small white room.

"I really don't look like this. Please can you get me back to the person I was?" I begged the doctor as I desperately searched in my pocket for my phone and scrambled through photographs until I found one of me – of how I was before.

"That's me," I said tearfully. "Not this." I hung my head in shame.

"We've no idea why the swelling has got this bad, Camille," said the doctor. "So we're going to carry out some tests to try to figure this out, ok?"

I felt a sense of relief because I knew these people could take care of me and fix things. They'd run some tests, find out the problem and fix it.

It turned out my inflammatory markers were off the charts. That's all they would tell me at first. So I was handed some anti-inflammatories to help the swelling go down.

I sat on the crumpled white bed sheets wearing a flimsy hospital gown and, over the course of many hours, a stream of different doctors came in, each of them taking a sample of blood or performing one test or another. Then off they'd go, footsteps getting quieter as they disappeared down the corridor. Each time I heard the footsteps returning I'd sit up, hopeful for some news. But the footsteps would disappear again and I'd be left with my fear and thoughts racing around my swollen head.

Finally a doctor came in. Perhaps now I'd get some answers. They told me the swelling was due to my eczema, probably caused by my contracting a virus and my skin, given that it was covered in open wounds, becoming infected. The open cuts coupled with a 20% deficiency in zinc, the healing mineral, meant my body was susceptible to getting ill and had a very limited immune system, so my skin couldn't bind together and heal.

"Look, I'm really sorry Camille, you're in adulthood now, you're 21 and, I'm sorry to say, you've not grown out of your eczema," said the doctor. He stood up. "The best-case-scenario for you now is to take a combination of internal steroids and anti-depressants to help you cope with it." And off he went, footsteps stepping away from me and my life-long problem.

I sat staring at the place where the doctor had been standing, thinking, "So this is it? This is my fate? I have to look like this, feel like this, take excruciating showers, watch my hair continue to fall out. And this is going to be my life now?"

I hadn't been fixed. Instead I'd been given a life sentence.

Of course I didn't want to take the steroids or anti-depressants. I didn't want to feel depressed. Nobody does. And I didn't want to feel depressed and look awful. The worse I looked, the worse I felt. The worse I felt, the worse my eczema became. But over the years I'd developed such a fear of steroid creams and drugs that I wouldn't even take a tablet for a headache.

the beginning

I cast my mind back to being a little girl, when I was first diagnosed with eczema, age six. I remember being covered in Sudocrem and wrapped in bandages. My grandma knitted me mittens to stop me scratching at night, but I habitually pulled them off in my sleep. I'd look at my siblings and wonder why I was the only one with this. Perhaps I'd done something wrong and was being punished?

"Grandad," I'd say. "Am I ugly?"

He was shocked to hear me say that and asked me why I thought such a thing? "Because I have eczema and bandages."

He reassured me. "You won't have it forever," he said.

But here I was two decades later being told in no uncertain terms that yes, I would.

school days

As I grew older, my eczema began to bother me more. I remember when I was 13, I wanted to hide it from my classmates and my hands often hurt when I typed on the keyboard. So I'd wear gloves to computer class to provide some comfort and prevent anyone from seeing my ghastly hands. Of course, my classmates quizzed me about why I was wearing them and the teacher shouted at me to remove them.

When I peeled them off, the boy sitting next to me who was a friend of mine noticed the cuts all over my hands. He thought I was self-harming, but I told him I had a condition which meant I scratched myself at night. He didn't understand. How could he? I certainly didn't. All I knew was that it got worse in the winter as my skin cracked open due to the cold weather and central heating.

On the whole though, I hid how much my skin bothered me, choosing instead to focus on whatever made me happy, such as art and sport. Painting and making scrapbooks gave me the chance to express myself, while cross country running made me feel free. My worries about my skin faded with each step I ran.

I wasn't the popular girl at high school. In fact, there was a particular group of girls who didn't like me and they'd make sure I knew it; telling me to not to go into school the next day through MSN Chat.

I ignored them and instead focused on being chosen for the athletics team, because I relished the freedom from worries that running gave me. Being the youngest in the team and running with the years above me, I was too shy to talk to them on the bus. But I thought, perhaps if I won my races for our team, they might talk to me. They did something else instead.

On the way to the running events, they'd break packets of crisps up and pour them all over my head. Little mouse me didn't have the confidence to ask them to stop, so I just sat there with crisps on my head, thinking, 'It's fine. I'm going to win my race and they're going to like me.' So off I'd speed on the running track, winning the race by a whole lap. Everyone cheered, so I thought 'Yay! No more crisps on the head.' Onto the bus I hopped, sat down and felt and smelt the familiar feeling of crisps being poured on me.

Sometimes, during puberty, my eczema would get so unbearably bad, I couldn't face going to school at all. It would flare up overnight and my lips would be so swollen, I couldn't even move my mouth.

So I'd cry and plead with mum to let me stay home so I could stay in bed all day to sleep and heal. But having all this time off made me feel incredibly isolated and insecure.

Here I was, a 15 year old, about to go off to boarding school with the world at my feet. I wanted to be the netball captain, I wanted to learn and travel, but this condition was controlling me. I desperately wanted to regain control.

As a child I loved the doctors, because they'd take all my problems away, so as I grew older I'd beg them to give me penicillin and steroid creams. However, while the combination of these drugs helped heal my skin initially, it never lasted. I'd need a stronger dose of medication each time, and I was becoming reliant on them.

I soon realised that my uncle, who also suffered from terrible eczema, had been using steroids for decades, yet his skin was still red raw. Not only that, despite the medication, my eczema kept returning. It was relentless. I needed something that would get rid of this permanently rather than temporarily.

prevention

That's when something clicked in my head, and I realised prevention would be better than temporary cure. The creams were a temporary solution. I needed to figure out a way to stop using these drugs. I needed to find an alternative solution. And I needed to figure out what was causing my eczema in the first place.

Besides, at boarding school I'd have nowhere to hide. I couldn't take days off to stay in bed, and I didn't want my new friends to see me like this in the evenings. I wanted it gone completely.

Subsequently, I became fascinated with the natural health industry vs the medical industry. The more I researched, the more natural remedies just made more sense to me, as they existed long before the medical industry. I realised the world has given us all we need to be healthy.

a fresh start

My research into natural remedies was interrupted during the school holidays as the family relocated to my parents house in France for a long summer. We spent our time outside surrounded by vineyards, eating from the fresh markets and soaking up the sun. It turned out nature was the ultimate medicine – when I started boarding school, my skin was glowing. The combination of the sunshine, salty sea, happiness and relaxing vibes must have helped heal my skin.

I loved starting a new school and cherished the chance to have a fresh start and to meet new people. My skin continued to glow. Things were looking up.

I had an amazing circle of supportive friends and there was a wonderful sense of camaraderie as we became each other's family. Healthy meals were reasonably accessible and I was doing sport everyday; going on daily runs with my best friend and becoming netball captain. I was in my element and loving school. Everything slotted neatly into place. Life was great, and so was my skin.

It must have been January when my eczema began to flare up due to the colder weather and the prospect of exams looming.

I didn't want anyone to know I had this skin disease and was sick of having to cope with it, so I turned to my mum who was quite holistic herself. She took me to have a series of allergy tests which showed me all the foods and chemicals I was apparently intolerant to. She'd always insisted on giving me fish oils as a kid because it was good for my brain, so it made perfect sense that certain foods might be good (or bad) for my skin.

The list was long! So many foods and chemicals appeared on that A4 sheet, which included everything affecting my skin; everything I should avoid: tomatoes, oranges, gluten, dairy, even lettuce!

This was the first time I felt in control. I was determined never to eat or use anything listed on that crucial piece of paper ever again. I threw out all of my beauty products and became really strict with myself, severely restricting what I consumed. I handed the list to the school caféteria and refused to eat anything at home or school that had even the tiniest bit of tomato in it.

My drastic action seemed to work. My skin started glowing again, but I lost a lot of weight.

For the next two years I kept up this strict avoidance diet. I'd eat a banana for breakfast, chicken or fish with vegetables for lunch, and a bowl of peas or gluten-free cereal for dinner – that was it. The problem was, because the list was so restrictive, I developed a fear of food. After a year of restriction it turned into an obsession, which became orthorexia – a medical condition where the sufferer systematically avoids specific foods they believe to be harmful.

Orthorexia didn't feel like a bad thing, though. Even though it had begun to control me, I still felt like I was in charge. Given that my skin condition had controlled my life for so long, I relished the fact that the control was now in my hands. If anyone questioned the way I ate, I stubbornly told them they weren't in a position to question me because, I reasoned, there was far more nutrition in my bowl of peas than in their pizza.

"This is who I am and this is what I'm going to eat," I declared, and if anyone told me otherwise or insisted I eat something that would make my eczema return, I'd get angry. They didn't know how that food affected me, and I didn't ever want to go back to having to wear gloves and isolate myself from everyone to heal. And I didn't want to take any drugs either.

Of course, what I failed to realise at the time was that I wasn't eating healthily because I wasn't eating enough. I would get incredibly tired and go to bed as early as 7pm some nights, straight after finishing my studies. This was partly due to tiredness, and partly because I knew staying awake would make it difficult to avoid eating. So I became less social, more controlled and obsessive. At the time I thought I was doing the best thing for myself, but I was in an avoid zone, rather than a nourish zone. I focused on 'What I Can't Eat' rather than 'What I Can Eat' – and that's not a positive way to live.

Research on setting goals has shown that they are far healthier (and easier to stick to) if they are 'approach' goals rather than 'avoidance' goals.

However, sticking to this restrictive diet made me much thinner and, given that we live in a world which celebrates slenderness, it felt like I was being validated externally for being thin; rewarded for my own avoidance. My skin was glowing and I loved being slim, because I dreamt of becoming a model. I thought I was on track, nothing else mattered. I didn't see the negative side or realise that I'd developed an unhealthy fear of food. All I cared about was that denying myself food was helping to keep my eczema at bay.

Or was it?

Once I started to study business management at Bath University, my eczema returned. It was fresher's week, so there was lots of alcohol and partying. I was still obsessive about food, so would eat very little and eat my meals alone as I didn't want to feel uncomfortable about what I was eating.

Of course, being university, I couldn't avoid going out completely, but I was exhausted from the lack of food and level of alcohol. Not only that, but business management simply wasn't my passion. I had taken the course on as my dad advised that studying business would leave my future open to all avenues in life. He had worked his way up from nothing and become a successful businessman, so I respected his advice. I wasn't particularly interested in the course, being more of a creative person, and I didn't know anyone in the area.

Where everything had slotted into place so neatly at boarding school, here I felt like every little piece that did fit, suddenly didn't. Chaos ensued.

Instinctively I'd skip lectures and read nutrition books, cut out more foods and try my best to heal. But I was falling behind in my studies. I didn't want to let anyone down, so I tried some other courses, from graphic design and writing to media, but everyone else had done a foundation course or was further ahead, so none of them felt right. I even tried a food and nutrition course, but they were teaching how to make bread with gluten in. I couldn't be in a class surrounded by food I couldn't eat.

Eventually I quit university altogether. I was initially too embarrassed to tell my dad that I couldn't cope on the course he recommended so, before opening up, I got myself a job in a bar to prove I could support myself. Of course, once he heard the news, he insisted I come home. He initially suggested I work for him until I got onto another university course, but I persuaded him to let me heal my skin before starting afresh.

With the stress and chaos of university gone, my regular gym visits, time to relax and strict diet helped me to heal my eczema again. I even applied to be the model of LoveLula. When they hired me, I was over the moon; becoming the face of LoveLula was my dream come true. I also applied for a more creative course in marketing and brand management, which felt like a better fit. Once again I felt good about life, and my skin felt good too.

But it wasn't to last. Back at a new university, despite drinking 'clear' alcohol (like vodka and cranberry or gin and tonic), I'd have the occasional shot and my eczema soon returned. Once again, it prevented me from doing what I wanted to do. My eczema dictated everything. I wanted to be a cheerleader, but the squad had cheer socials every Wednesday. I wanted to do netball, but the socials were all about getting as drunk as possible and less about the sport. I just couldn't participate, despite my friends' pleas for me to come and party with them.

Going out without drinking wasn't enjoyable for me either, as you're on a completely different wavelength and feel just as isolated as you do when you're home alone, so I needed to do something else. I couldn't drop out of university again. There had to be another option.

That's when I discovered the study abroad programme, which enabled students to go abroad for a year of their course. I applied for California, but was offered New York. Knowing how cold it can get there, I declined, reapplied and got California the second time around. It was like the stars had aligned for me, at last. For my second year at university, I could go to California. I just needed to persuade my dad.

It took me that whole first year at uni to convince him to let me go, because he thought I was too young to live abroad. Then, on my 20th birthday, he asked me what I wanted. I told him what I wanted more than anything was to have his approval to go to California. Thankfully, he agreed under the proviso that I had proven this was what I wanted and that he trusted me to take care of myself. I was free to go!

the sunshine state

And wow! What a difference! At university in California hardly anyone I knew drank alcohol, and if they did, it was nowhere near as much as we did at my English uni. I bonded with friends, taking Pilates classes and touring the State. We would visit botanical gardens, climb to the Hollywood sign, go on road trips, study by the pool, snowboard. We participated in so many exciting activities that fed my soul and didn't involve alcohol. And my new friends loved how much I wanted to embrace the California vibe.

It was uplifting to find people doing something worthwhile; I felt like I had found my people. Of course, going to concerts sober took a bit of getting used to at first. The legal age to drink was 21 and I was still only 20. But it was such a delight to have fun without alcohol and I enjoyed people knowing me for me, rather than the drunk version of myself. I ran everyday and I enjoyed the course on Change Management I was doing. I was absolutely in my element.

What's more, I felt accepted here. I had a sense of belonging that I'd only ever experienced at boarding school. All the pieces of my life fitted into place, just as they had back then. And, once more, my skin was glowing.

According to scientific research, we need to feel like we belong. Belonging is a vital component for human happiness. Meanwhile, the field of positive psychology has come up with pillars of wellbeing which are like the pieces of a jigsaw puzzle. We need all the pieces to fit in order to really flourish in our lives. No wonder my skin was glowing during the periods of my life where the pieces fit together, where I felt like I belonged. I was creating the conditions for thriving – mentally and physically.

However, I didn't realise that fitting the jigsaw pieces together was the key to sustainable healing and wellbeing until much later. At the time I was still convinced my healing was down to what we put into our bodies via the food and drink we consumed.

So, I poured over books about juicing. I also read a book by Polly Noble and thought: if she can heal herself from cancer, there's hope for me to heal from eczema.

I loved learning as I soaked up the sunshine and the warm vibes of the people I surrounded myself with.

The problem was, I couldn't stay in California forever. I needed to return home in the autumn, as I'd found myself a year-long internship at a health company, which I saw as a great way to continue living my healthy lifestyle. But, when my brother invited me to his sixth form ball in June, I didn't want to let him down. My family mean the world to me and I knew being at his ball would mean a lot to him. So I travelled home early as soon as my course in California ended.

going backwards

Travelling back to the UK felt like travelling back in time. Catching up with everyone made me realise how much more 'myself' I felt out in California. But there was no point in dwelling, as I was here now. I threw myself into getting organised, rushing around trying to find a house in Bicester so I could move into it in time to start my new internship job. My sister had also found a new job, so we decided to get a house in between where we each had to commute to. It was all-go and I was running on juice, quite literally. I'd run in the mornings and became obsessed with juicing, to the point of hardly eating any real meals.

In California I'd found myself and I'd found happiness. When I finally came up for air, I realised the bubble of happiness had burst. Before long, my eczema returned. I told myself it was the stress of moving house and doing so much, and picked myself up by reminding myself about the exciting new internship for a health company. I believed that if I kept on juicing everyday, I'd be sure to nip this flare-up of eczema in the bud, right?

when the dream turns into a nightmare

The commute and the internship really took their toll. The commute meant I was getting up early, going to bed late, and feeling too tired and stressed to run in the mornings. Scratching at night meant I wasn't sleeping. But this was my dream internship and I wasn't about to let my eczema spoil it.

I threw myself into the job, but my boss asked me what was happening to my skin. He wanted to know why my eczema was coming back. His company hadn't been offering internships when I applied. I'd just been so determined to find an inspirational company to work for, I'd contacted him directly and asked for an internship. At my interview, I'd explained how much of a healthy lifestyle I led, how I juiced every single day. But here I was doing my dream internship, and the lack of sleep was really affecting me. I tried to hold it together, but felt like the worst intern.

At weekends the marketing director would ask me to work and, despite the exhaustion, I'd agree to do so. I hardly saw my boyfriend, because I was either working or commuting. And, apart from juicing, I wasn't taking care of myself at all. I'd wake up in sheets full of blood and skin and my then-boyfriend would dress me and wrap my hands in bandages just to go to work. Driving there became increasingly painful.

Not only was my poor sleep and worsening eczema causing an issue, not knowing what I was doing made the job itself confusing. I had no marketing experience and wasn't given any guidance about what I should be doing. As it was the first proper job I'd ever had, I was expecting to learn. But all I learnt was that the reality of a dream job can be very far from your expectations.

I had no clue what was expected of me and no idea what I was doing, so I felt completely lost and under pressure. I ended up doing random tasks that were asked of me, from cutting the hedge to making coffees, neither of which I'd done before. I was a naive non-coffee-drinking intern who was so oblivious to real-life scenarios in a working environment, I felt utterly out of my depth.

It also confused me that nobody in the office was healthy. I was working for this leading health firm and there I was with my juice, while everyone else was off to get their coffees. I felt like an outsider who didn't fit in.

At that young age it can be difficult to say, 'I'm not sure what I should be doing'. Asking for help can feel weak. I also assumed that everyone else totally knew what they were doing all the time. Of course, that's something I've subsequently realised isn't the case; we all have imposter syndrome from time to time and feel like we're going to be found out at any moment. But I didn't see that then. I just felt like a duck out of water. On top of that, having such terrible skin whilst juicing and working for a company which promoted that healthy lifestyle made me feel even more like a fraud.

I'd been looking forward to this internship for so long, I was distraught about this lack of synergy with working in the health industry. But I wasn't about to give up. So I used my own initiative and gave myself tasks to do. My boss had brought out some new health-food bars which he wanted in different stores, so I rang up all the stores I thought might stock them, asking to speak to the manager and inviting them to stock our bars. I tried to do all I could to impress the people who worked there, as it felt like nobody really wanted me there. I just didn't click with anyone.

I also decided to work on giving a talk about juicing to schools, but I was in so much pain I thought: 'Who am I to speak about this? Look at me!' Despite cutting out gluten and sugar and regularly juicing, my skin still wasn't healthy. That was my first awakening that you can eat and drink healthily, but will still have eczema when everything else is out of balance.

And the fact that I didn't click with anyone presented me with more evidence to demonstrate the importance of having all the pieces of the jigsaw of life fitting together. During this internship I felt out of my depth, like I didn't belong and I wasn't eating a balanced diet as I was living on juice. The pieces didn't fit and I was stressed, tired and disappointed. No wonder my eczema flared up.

my desperate flee to the dead sea

I was swimming out of my depth already, so when my boss, who had suffered from a skin disease himself, suggested I swim in Israel's Dead Sea, it didn't seem too drastic a solution. 'Why not?' I thought. He suggested I needed to have some time off, to heal my skin. "A good two weeks," he said.

So, one rainy day, I took myself off to the airport, boarded a plane, got a bus to a juice retreat in Israel and told the host of my plans."You're crazy," she said. "You have no idea how painful that's going to be. I don't recommend this." But I was determined to live off juice and go in the Dead Sea, just as my boss had done. I would rid myself of eczema once and for all, and prove to him I was worthy of working for him. "I don't care how painful it is," I declared. "I'm healing my skin."

On the sand I spotted a lot of people with skin problems, but everyone was splashing around in the sea, having fun, so in I went.

Walking into that sea was literally like pouring salt into an open wound. The burning pain was unbearable. It was like someone had set fire to my body, as I felt like I was being burned to death. But I would go to any lengths in an attempt to heal.

That first day I ran out of the sea towards the shower. A long queue of 20 people stood between me and the water that would wash away the burning pain. But I stood there patiently, shaking and crying. The people in line couldn't speak English, but they pushed me to the front of the queue and helped wash the salt water off me. They could see the intense pain I was in.

But I knew that salt water was very healing. So I was determined to keep going back in each day, even if I could only bear a few seconds at a time. I just kept telling myself, "This is it, this is the answer, this is going to heal me."

After the third day of being all alone in Israel, living purely on juice and not having any food, I burst into tears on the phone to my mum and asked her to come out for the second week. It was so isolating here, I couldn't do this alone. Thankfully, my dad was working hard supporting us all financially, so it meant mum could be with me for as long as I needed her.

Mum arrived and managed to get me to eat. Her support gave me the strength I needed. And, by the end of the second week, I could actually lie in the water for 30 minutes and my skin began to heal.

On the last day in Israel, I messaged my boss to tell him how much better I was, how I was ready to come back and how I'd been studying the books he'd suggested I read.

Moments later, as I sat in my hotel room, the fan whirring ominously, an e-mail pinged. It was a message from my boss telling me they didn't want me to come back, that I wasn't what I sold myself as, and that it wasn't worth them having me there.

But I'd fixed the problem – and endured next-level pain in order to do so! I'd done exactly as my boss had suggested and it had worked. Had I really been through all that pain for nothing? After all I'd endured, I just broke down. I couldn't believe I'd lost my job because of this stupid condition!

Sadly, I flew home and, within two days of returning from Israel, eczema was everywhere again.

lost

I felt so let down. This was supposed to be my year of gaining work experience and I desperately needed to finish my internship in order to complete my university course, to which I'd be returning for my final year the following September. I felt like such a failure and a liability and didn't want to go back to my dad, cap in hand, to ask for his support, when all I wanted was to make him proud.

But, as I wasn't being paid to work, he offered to help me financially. He'd prefer me to work for him and get a proper guided internship, but I wanted to be able to eventually stand on my own two feet and gain experience in the health industry. I didn't want to always be reliant on him for a job or money – as much as I appreciated how privileged I was, I wanted to prove myself and earn in an industry that I loved. I wanted to prove how capable I was of becoming successful in my own right and to take the weight off his shoulders, so he didn't always feel he needed to work so hard to support me.

So, when I was told not to come back to work, I didn't let it lie. I begged my boss to let me work at no cost to him with the marketing director, Kris, who was only in the office two days a week and, the rest of the time, worked from home in Swindon. If Kris would let me work from his Swindon home office, I could finish my internship and complete my studies. My sister was commuting to Swindon, so perhaps we could kill two birds with one stone and move there together? My boss reluctantly agreed and, given that the commute had been taking its toll on both of us, my sister and I both moved to Swindon at the end of December.

Despite this fresh start, I was still struggling that things hadn't worked out as I'd hoped, and still ruminating on the painful trip to Israel and losing my initial internship as a result of my eczema. In Swindon it was quite lonely, as my only work 'colleague' was Kris, and my sister and boyfriend weren't around much.

The isolation continued and I couldn't help but compare my life now to my life in California. I also felt guilty that I was relying on my dad to pay my half of the bills as my internship didn't pay. I had lost my way and my eczema continued.

Christmas came and went and, as I scratched my way through the nights, I felt myself burning up. I thought I was reliving my Dead Sea experience, but I'd caught a virus and reacted so badly to it, I ended up sat on a hospital bed in tears, being told I'd have this skin disease forever.

enough

Back home from hospital I rang my mum. My chest heaved up and down from sobbing, my face was blotchy from the combination of tears and raw eczema and my voice croaky from crying so much.

It was then that I shut off from the world. I'd had enough. I'd lost all faith. I didn't know what my reason for living was. I was in so much pain, and, because I'd refused to let anyone in, I felt like I had no friends, no career. I remember feeling like I didn't want to wake up any more. I was done. I didn't see the point in sharing my problem with anyone, because nobody could solve it. I couldn't, so how could anyone else? There was no point confiding in anyone.

I felt like a rubbish friend, a rubbish family member, a rubbish intern. I felt like I'd let everyone down and that it'd be better for everyone if I disappeared.

"I don't want to be here any more," I said to my mum who, crushed by hearing those words come from her child, decided to come down south to stay with me and help me recover from this deep depression I'd sunk into.

The next day I picked myself up, dusted myself off, went on a run and drank my juice. I was still convinced that was all that would work, despite all the evidence to the contrary. Healing is about more than food and exercise. I didn't want to take the anti-inflammatories, so my mum had to force me to take them. And they seemed to be working, until the evening came.

The night after I came out of hospital, the hot sweats worsened and my head began to swell again. My mum and my sister rushed me to hospital and pleaded with the doctors. Surely, this was more serious than they'd first thought. I saw my sister's fiery protective side come out. She wanted them to do something about it immediately. So she did care. I just hadn't been open to seeing how much, as I was so wrapped up in my own problems and fears.

Despite my sister's pleas, we waited hours before I was taken into a hospital room. Over the next few hours I heard the sound of the green curtain being pulled open and closed as doctors and nurses ran in and out, doing more tests. I hadn't eaten, but I couldn't eat the hospital food, so my mum fed me healthy juice and nuts when the doctors weren't looking and sat with me holding my hand. Once again, I was given the all-clear and sent home with anti-inflammatories and more steroids.

loving support

With some TLC and rest, the infection finally cleared up. Mum was my rock. If it hadn't been for her presence, love and support, what happened next wouldn't have happened. I would have remained a 'caterpillar' forever, lost in a loop of despair, convinced that food and exercise would heal me. I owe so much to her persistent love and care and to the support of my then-boyfriend who was also extremely caring during this painful time. Their combined love showed me how important supportive relationships are to the healing process. But I'd been intent on locking people out of my life, convinced they couldn't help me.

I remember saying to my boyfriend back then, 'Why are you with me? Look at me! I can't even look at myself.' I told him,'You've heard my fate, it's never going away, you should leave me now.' But he'd reassure me by telling me I'd get through this, that it wouldn't last forever, that I was still beautiful me on the inside. He'd hug me when I was falling asleep crying, he'd fetch me a cold flannel and fan me down if I was too hot or if I was scratching. He was such a good friend. But I've since learned we need a small network of support to really make a difference.

Between them and my friends and family who, once I'd opened up to them, rallied around, their constant support helped me transform from a lost and itchy caterpillar into a vibrant and joyful butterfly. After years of obsessing about juice, and exercise and fear of food I finally realised LOVING SUPPORT is just as medicinal and healing.

No, it wasn't the creams or the pills or even the diet and exercise – it was the combination of loving support and a shift in MINDSET that finally helped me to heal.

CHAPTER 2

Cocoon

In life, we often experience our toughest challenges before gaining our greatest rewards. Things have a habit of getting worse before they get better. This has certainly been true for me. Having endured one setback after another – from losing my internship and having my eczema return, despite my excruciating dip in the Dead Sea, to being told to give up hope of healing following my traumatic time in hospital – I felt trapped in my own skin.

Worse than that, I felt worthless, hopeless and utterly drained. Yet these events and emotions provided me with the first catalyst for change and, as such, the first springboard towards my healing journey.

With my mum's support, I refused to take this hopeless diagnosis as my fate and, with help, I emerged on the other side.

Sometimes I think we need to go through the bad to fully appreciate the good. I truly believe this.

In fact, I often wonder whether all of this was meant to happen so I could more fully appreciate where I am now. Would I have been so determined to help other people who are suffering now as I once was, had I not been through this? Had it not got so bad? Had I not hit absolute rock bottom?

My favourite quote is: "An arrow can only be shot by pulling it backward. So when life is dragging you back with difficulties, it means that it's going to launch you into something great." That's been so true when I look at my life. Had I not been pulled back to face adversities – from hospital admission to career drama and a troublesome night-time scratching habit – I wouldn't have discovered the strategies that have helped me to heal, nor would I have sought opportunities that have been incredibly great, such as my time in California (which I only discovered out of desperation, wanting to escape the cold climate).

Sometimes life doesn't always go the way you plan, but I believe it is always for our greatest good. It took me a long time to get over the eczema consuming my entire body, but now I can see that I went through this to help me realise just how strong I am. Now I have emerged on the other side, I can use my experiences to provide hope to others who are suffering like I once did.

What I know for sure is: had I not been told over and over, even by Harley Street doctors, that steroid cream and anti-depressants were the only viable solution, I wouldn't have sought an alternative. Had it not got so bad, I wouldn't have been willing to try a different approach, nor would I have discovered my zinc deficiency, which led to me switching up my food eating habits to become healthier and more balanced.

making changes

But, before I could emerge as a butterfly, I had to enter the cocoon stage. This focus on my self-care acted as my final preparation towards the healing that I had long yearned for.

Cocoons feel like safe places. Yet darkness still surrounds you. And so this was true for me. But, on hearing that I should take anti-depressants and steroids for the foreseeable future, I realised that I didn't want to numb it, I didn't want to be ok with this, I didn't want to accept it as my fate. In this way I felt strangely glad that I wasn't alright, because it made me want to do something about it. It made we want to take action. Being consciously aware of my eczema and the perpetual pain I was in led me to be active rather than passive; to take the lead rather than follow the same old advice I'd been given for years, which simply wasn't helping.

I knew I needed to do something different.

As Albert Einstein once said, 'Insanity is doing the same thing over and over again and expecting different results.'

Doing the same thing over and over – the creams, the tablets, even the diets, had led me to being hospitalised and to shut down. After hospital I didn't know what my reason for living was. I was in so much pain, I felt like I had no friends (not their fault – I just hadn't let them in, because I was too scared to). I had no career. I just didn't want to wake up any more.

Thankfully I had someone in my corner who, when I told them I didn't want to be here, took action on my behalf. She battled with my stubborn nature until I accepted that maybe, just maybe, her suggestions might be worth trying.

She bought me a book called *The Secret*. At first I refused to read it, but she insisted that we needed to change my mindset, and she knew this book beautifully demonstrates how powerful our thoughts can be in attracting into our lives whatever it is we are thinking (or worrying or obsessing) about.

"This isn't the Camille I know," she said. "You were so happy a year ago."

Once again my mind flashed back to the sunnier happier times in California, and my desperate longing to feel that way again spurred me into action. She insisted that she had a plan and that we would be following it.

"This is NOT going to be your fate," she told me and I nodded, happy to have someone taking control of the situation.

mind over matter

Mum had heard about NLP (Neuro-Linguistic Programming) and said she really wanted me to speak to someone about it. Of course, I didn't want to at first. After all, this was an actual proper condition! It had nothing to do with what was going on in my head. It was real and I was living it. The idea that I could control it with my mind seemed illogical and, to be honest, a little bit offensive. It was like suggesting it was all in my head, as if I'd made it happen.

But I decided to humour my mum. Here she was offering her support and love – the least I could do was go along with what she suggested. It certainly couldn't make things any worse.

Before she booked an appointment, she made me write down ten things I was grateful for about my life right now. If I wrote anything that wasn't good enough, she made me write them out again.

At first I couldn't think of anything to be grateful for.

Life was bleak.

A friendless, jobless, hopeless mess.

But I was focusing my attention on what I lacked, rather than what I had.

"Camille," she would say, "you have legs, you can walk."

So I'd begrudgingly jot that down.

"Look at you Camille! You can still go for a run!"

And she was right. Even on my darkest days I still pushed myself to go out for a run. So I wrote down how grateful I was for my fitness.

I was grateful to have such a supportive boyfriend who loved me for me. I was grateful to be so close to my family.

I had been resentful that my sister was able to go out partying and eat pizza and junk food, while I juiced and ate healthily but was the one who was ill. Then I remembered how she'd demonstrated how much she cared during my time in hospital, so I wrote that down:

"I'm so lucky to have such a supportive sister."

Once I began, gratitude poured out.

"I'm grateful for my drive." I had been feeling devastated that I wasn't achieving my ambitions, but the fact that I had some drive inside me was something to feel thankful for, so I added 'my ambition' to my gratitude list.

Each day mum would make me read out my gratitude list, so I'd become grateful for all that I had, despite what I was going through. Shifting my focus in this way was a turning point.

Before long, this process of writing down everything I had to be grateful for made me realise I wasn't as badly off as I thought. In fact, I was quite lucky.

Hmmm. Maybe this mindset shifting thing wasn't such a bad idea after all. That said, I was still uncertain about taking it a step further. I was starting to feel a little lighter and more hopeful about the future, but it wasn't stopping me scratching every night, waking up covered in blood and crying in pain every morning in the shower.

I was still experiencing dark times amid the light.

My cocoon was safe yet dark.

That's why I wanted answers. How could I stop myself from scratching every night? I just didn't understand. I was eating healthy foods.

"You're not going to live the rest of your life like this," said mum. "We're going to find a way."

So she made some phone calls and, despite my protests, mum being mum, she passed the phone to me and insisted I spoke to the NLP practitioner on the end of the line.

The following day I spent an hour with him and he unpicked everything that had happened with work, moving home from California, going into hospital. First of all he listened intently, as everything poured out of me like a waterfall flowing after a dam had burst. He helped me acknowledge how I was feeling about returning to the UK, and reassured me that it was okay to feel the way I did about my skin, my work and my family situation. He explained that he felt like I was trapped in my own body and the situation I'd found myself in, but that he was going to help me rewire how I felt about all that had happened, which helped me see how I could move forward.

reframing

We put a positive spin on every single negative judgement I had about my situation and each experience I'd been through.

That night was the first time I had slept in a very long time!

It was like all the pressure of the past few years had been lifted; like a heavy weight I'd been carrying around my neck had been removed. All that I was wrangling with had been taken off my hands, unwound and smoothed out. I felt organised and capable for the first time in a long while as I realised: 'Yes, I can do this'.

My transformation had begun; my head unscrambled.

Each negative hindering thought was reframed and replaced with a new, more helpful one. For example, when I said, 'I miss California', he asked me to replace that thought with 'One day I'll return to California. It's not gone forever'. When I said, 'I'm so ugly now', 'My boyfriend is bound to leave me' and 'None of my friends will like me', he'd give me affirmations such as: 'I am beautiful. My eyes are beautiful', 'My boyfriend loves me for who I am on the inside', 'My friends will support me once I let them in', and 'Now I believe I'm still beautiful, my skin will heal'.

When I expressed concerns about letting my family down, he suggested, 'I love my family and support them in my own way'. And, 'No matter what happens, my family will always love me'. Anything I was stressing about, he painted a picture of it all being okay eventually.

When I said, 'I'm trapped here' or 'I'm never going to get a job', he wrote an affirmation that said something to the contrary, such as, 'I'm an intelligent, talented and educated young woman'. 'I'm capable of any job I want to do', and 'I will earn enough income to help me move abroad one day and support me in life'.

At first I questioned him. Did he really think I'd be able to do that? To heal and find work and garner support? My confidence had been so sorely dented by my disastrous internship, I had no faith in myself or my abilities any more. Yet he told me calmly and firmly that yes, he believed I could. In fact, he was sure of it.

And his belief was contagious.

He'd given me a different way of seeing things, a different lens through which to see the world.

I was now fully equipped with a list of positive affirmations:

- "I am in the right place, at the right time, doing the right thing."
- "I approve of myself."
- "I am beautiful."
- "I am healthy, happy and well and my skin is glowing."

My homework was to wake up each day, look in the mirror and repeat these affirmations out loud – an incredibly difficult process. I'd been avoiding looking in the mirror for so long. And if I did ever happen to catch my reflection, I'd see anxious sad eyes staring back at me and I'd look away.

But I pressed on, determined to make this work. And, before long, I started to believe what I was saying.

Yes, I was capable. Yes, I could do this. Yes, I was worthy.

The affirmations became self-fulfilling prophecies, just as the negative thoughts had done previously.

Back then, when I told myself I was unworthy of friendships and didn't let them in, my friends got on with their lives. Back then, when I told myself I was never going to escape this condition, I continued to scratch and my eczema remained.

But now, when I started to say 'my friends support me' and began to let my friends in, they were devastated that I hadn't told them and they gave me more support and encouragement than I ever gave them credit for. I was able to replace my belief that 'nobody can help me, I'm on my own' with 'I can trust people around me, because they all want the best for me'.

The fact I had started sleeping meant I started healing, which made me more positive and gave me more energy. Wrapping myself up in a cocoon of self-love and sleep and positivity was working wonders.

My arm would still reach to scratch. But my boyfriend would gently move my arm and stop me. If I persisted he'd get put a cold flannel on the area and, because I was sleeping, the areas I wasn't scratching were healing. From then on, if I did wake myself scratching, I'd force my arm off, put a cool flannel on and apply the pressure myself.

I had lots of mental willpower during the day. Nothing would make me scratch. In the evenings, I'd let go and have no control. But, once I kept feeding myself these positive thoughts, I didn't have as much urge to scratch. It was still there, but less prevalent. And now, five years on, I just don't scratch at all.

But here's the thing I've learned about willpower and mental energy. We have more willpower in the morning because our willpower-o-meter is full. Each time we use it, we use our reserves of willpower until, by the time it's night-time, we've used it up and have depleted our mental energy. That's why we need to equip ourselves sufficiently with tools to help us. Positivity helped me to sleep, which, combined with the strategy of using a cold flannel to reduce the itching sensation, helped me to heal. But positivity did more than give my willpower and sleep a boost. It gave me a new lease of life.

It was like I'd been handed a permission slip to go forth and do whatever it took to heal.

That permission empowered me to change my way of thinking, to feel differently about situations and challenges. I realised I was entitled to carve out the life I wanted for myself and had the capability to do so, whatever the state of my skin.

My life was there for me to claim.

Mum and I sat down together and wrote a business plan for my dream business – one where I would help people, like me, who were suffering from eczema and at their wits' end.

"Step one – Heal myself. Get rid of my eczema," I wrote.

"Step two – finish university degree."

"Step three – find a website builder," and so on.

I was still covered head to toe in this terrible condition, but the shift in mindset gave me permission to dream and be hopeful. I wasn't going to let my eczema stand in the way of my dream to create a platform that would help people and make a real difference to their lives.

Mum got all the colouring pens out and, together, we drew up this plan. It was something we both believed in and her encouragement that 'yes, you can do this' further compounded my own belief in the idea and in myself and my abilities to bring it to fruition.

A couple of weeks earlier I'd been sitting in that hospital room, feeling hopeless. And here I was now feeling hopeful. This simple act of putting it out there into the Universe gave me hope and empowered me to believe that it was possible. I had something to aim for.

Of course, achieving that first step, of healing myself, wasn't going to be easy. But I already felt better after a good night's sleep, so I felt capable of taking it one day at a time, one step at a time, and I began to document what happened each day.

Being proactive about the management of my eczema by keeping a list to record whatever I'd done or experienced each day was so helpful. This eventually became a checklist, which helped me during flare-ups, as I could trace my finger down the list and figure out what might have caused the flare-up, what the triggers were and what I might be able to do about it.

Being proactive in this way helped me feel back in control.

And it gave me the evidence I needed to reveal that my recovery wasn't all about diet – it was about a whole lot more than that. By recording a true account of each experience and trigger, I began to see a different picture to the one I'd previously painted.

The missing zinc

Of course, food still played a part in my recovery. As well as booking my appointment with the NLP practitioner, mum had booked me an appointment to have some blood tests. I had eight vials of blood taken and felt dizzy and emotional, but it was worth it because I discovered I was 20% deficient in zinc. That was important to know because, without zinc, your immune system can't work properly, your skin can't heal, and you are mentally lower. This all made perfect sense and explained why my healing journey had felt like an uphill struggle.

At the time I was vegan, because I didn't want to eat animal products, not even fish, and I was having a reaction to nuts and seeds. Zinc is generally found in nuts, seeds, and meat. So, I wasn't getting any zinc, despite my healthy diet.

At first I started taking a zinc supplement, but the guy who ran the tests suggested I try to eat some meat. I'd been telling myself for so long that eating chicken and beef would not be good for me, so it was difficult to do so. But, as soon as I ate some chicken I started to regain energy, and things did change.

Adding chicken, a zinc supplement, a vitamin B supplement for mood-boosting and a probiotic to help my good bacteria made a real difference to my healing process because my skin was able to heal faster.

Had I not been admitted to hospital, my family may not have seen the need to get my blood tested and I wouldn't have known about my zinc deficiency. This proves to me that good things do come from bad things, so I'm appreciative of what happened now, because a lot of life-changing skin-healing good came from it.

Meanwhile, following my time in hospital, Kris (my manager from the health company where I had started my internship) had taken me under his wing to help him set up a juice bar in Swindon. I loved working for Kris. I got to do all the admin, create the juice bar and do all the design work. Going to work became a pleasurable experience, rather than a stressful one.

support

By March, although I was still suffering from eczema, it was starting to heal. As the spring began to sow its annual seeds of hope, I made an important discovery, which gave me even more hope for the future.

I learned the power and importance of supportive relationships.

A new girl called Katie had started working for Kris. She was lovely and we got on brilliantly. Within a week of knowing her, she'd bought me crystals to provide comfort. That simple act of kindness and support made such a difference. Plus, going into work with Katie was a joy. We became each other's sidekick as we were on the same wavelength and both liked eating healthy food. She was a part-time model and kept encouraging me that I could be a model too; perhaps we could even model together one day. It felt so good to have a friend to confide in again; someone who saw me for who I was.

I gained courage from her support and I took responsibility for myself. I told Kris I couldn't work late so that I had sufficient time to wind down and get to sleep. I started cooking more and eating more, now I had Katie as a friend. Things slowly started to come together and my eczema began to heal.

Meanwhile, my sister was launching a clothing brand called Avoid and had invited me to be the face of it. Back in February I had thanked her, but politely suggested she pick someone else, as I was still eczema-ridden. But my sister was defiant and said that by March it would all be gone, and that I would be the face of her brand.

People believed in me. My sister believed in me. And her belief in my healing helped me to believe in it too.

By March my eczema wasn't totally gone, but it was minimal enough for my sister to say 'Right, you're modelling for me'. So I did the photo shoot and my confidence grew again. I was on the road to healing. Modelling for her brand gave me confidence to be around people again too. Her support acted as a springboard towards accepting support from others.

A couple of months earlier I had positively affirmed in my gratitude list: 'I have a supportive sister', and here, once again, my positive affirmation was coming true.

It was around then I had an epiphany. From the safety of my cocoon it dawned on me that eczema was my body signalling to me that something wasn't right. I realised then that, even though I was eating a little more, it wasn't that different to the diet I'd had before my hospital admission. That's how I made the correlation between what worked for reducing my eczema and what didn't. I learned that it wasn't just about food and exercise – it was about lifestyle and support, belonging, acceptance, stress management, positive mindset and a whole bunch of things.

Now that I had the time to step back and examine the broader picture, I realised it wasn't about putting all my energy into exercise and diet. Because, if the other parts of the puzzle didn't fit, it'd be a waste of time. As a result, my checklist grew to include all these other areas of life too.

puzzle pieces fitting together

As one piece of the puzzle slotted into place, so did the next. While I was working for Kris I met Polly Noble, one of my health idols whose book I'd read whilst in California.

Polly wanted to put her food brand in the new juice bar I was helping Kris set up. She asked if any of us wanted to learn to cook.

I, of course, raised my hand.

That April, I became the raw chef and admin manager for the juice bar. It was wonderful to step away from the laptop and do something creative, and it was amazing to get to work with Polly – one of the nicest, most genuine people I've ever met.

As a result of these pieces of the puzzle coming together, my eczema reduced further. And I remember the immense gratitude I felt that Polly had not only walked into my life, but had taken me on to do all the food for her brand.

She saw past my eczema, and saw my capabilities and my enthusiasm instead. She invited me to be the chef for her brand and we became firm friends. Her positive vibes rubbed off on me.

The whole experience made me believe in serendipity and cemented this notion that setbacks are sometimes necessary as precursors for greater things. For, had I not been let go from the first health food company, I never would have ended up working for the Juice Bar and wouldn't have had the opportunity to meet, let alone work for, Polly Noble.

All of that heartache about losing my initial internship was worth it. Because who knew this is how it would end up – working in a job I loved with one of my health idols who greatly inspired me every single day? It just goes to show that stressing and worrying over circumstances beyond our control is futile, as we never know what good fortune is around the corner.

I truly believe that this was no coincidence. The work I'd been doing on my positive mindset had created a shift and I had begun to attract good situations and good people into my life. And, on top of that, my eczema was gradually healing.

Working with Polly also sparked a new passion inside me – cooking.

summer healing

As the summer arrived and the evenings grew lighter, my internship ended but, rather than feel sad or lost, I felt happy and equipped. I had learned so much, not only about the health food industry, raw cheffing and juicing, but about life itself – how a positive mindset and supportive relationships can feed your soul and heal your body.

My skin was almost completely clear again and I was excited about having the whole summer off, just doing the odd bit of admin work from my laptop for Polly.

My guy friends Danny, Dinnen and I headed off on a road trip to my parents' house in France. This was a turning point, the first trip I spent with my best friends after the hospital episode. It made me realise nothing had changed and, despite not letting them in for months, they still loved and cared for me. I stayed there all summer, which helped me prepare myself for my fourth and final year at university.

I spent that summer in France eating well, seeing friends, catching some rays and feeling like myself again – the version of me who had thrived in California was back. Perhaps I was emerging from my cocoon? I didn't wear any make up, jumped in and out of the sea, and picked fruit from our fruit garden. It was a treat to watch the figs grow and pick them, as soon as they were ripe, to make jam, which we'd give to my grandma.

The notion that nature was providing us with this beautiful gift which we could give to my grandma to spread on her toast – I loved that. That she could enjoy something I'd made from nature. That natural realness was very healing, like nature itself, and it sowed the seed for me to explore more natural skin healing methods. I also loved visiting the French markets and cooking food with my mum. That summer was a wonderful way to press pause and reset.

Of course, when I went back to university, I felt nervous again. But, mentally, I had changed. I was a completely different person to the naive young woman who had wanted to please everyone. Now my attitude was: 'This is who I am. I don't want to drink. I want to set up a business that's going to help people get rid of their eczema like I have, because I was told I couldn't, but I have.' That was my dream and my focus and I wasn't about to let anything get in my way; especially not eczema.

That said, I wasn't quite ready to emerge from my cocoon just yet. I had been through so much since I first started university, I wasn't about to make the same mistakes. So I focused on finishing my course, ramping up the self-care, exercising and keeping myself to myself. I rarely went out to party, preferring instead to cocoon myself in my room and have plenty of early nights.

The following spring I finished university and moved back home. After graduating with a 2:1 I started working as an assistant buyer for my dad's company so I could save some money. I already had the health company experience under my belt, but wanted to earn.

feeling the fear

Unfortunately, my mind hadn't completely healed because the fear was still there. I was starting to get anxious because my mind was telling me the story that whenever I moved home or went through a major life change, my eczema would return. So I was living in fear of that happening.

This anxiety about my eczema coming back meant I stopped sleeping well. And, sure enough, my thoughts became reality as, that winter, my eczema flared up a little. I started to have flashbacks to the trauma of my head swelling up. I think winter reminded me of that time, and it took me a long time to get over that.

As panic started to set in, I reached into my new toolkit to find the tools to help me. I booked myself in to see an NLP practitioner before my eczema flared up too much. I was determined to nip it in the bud.

However, despite the positive affirmations, I couldn't shake the fear or anxiety about my eczema coming back. I'd had enough of it controlling my life, but I had grown so used to it ruining everything that I had convinced myself that it would again. I remember crying so much in the practitioner's room; I was struggling to breathe as I explained how much fear I had of my eczema and hospital event returning. The event was long-gone, my skin had healed, yet I was still living in fear.

At the back of my mind, that fear still infiltrated everything: fear of food, fear of the wrong career, fear of looking back in that mirror and seeing my swollen head. The NLP practitioner tried to help me, but the cost of seeing her was out of my budget and I didn't want to tell my dad I was struggling again or ask for his financial support. So, I went home and my mum sat me down with an app called Headspace. She promised to do the meditation exercises with me every morning or evening until I started to sleep again.

pressing pause

Those short mindful pauses helped me become more mindful of my thoughts. And this, in turn, helped me to replace them with thoughts which served me better. I realised that while my mind was still racing with anxiety, it was no good saying positive affirmations as I hadn't found that calm head space. I needed to slow down and press pause first, by focusing on my breathing. Then I could use my positive affirmations in a calmer state of mind.

It was so important for me to equip myself with tools to handle not only the eczema itself and my management of it, but also my fears about it returning; especially because I now only had myself to rely on, especially at night time.

My boyfriend and I decided mutually to go our separate ways after university. He was living in Jersey, I was living up north again and, having had such an intense few years, we realised I needed the stability of one location for a while. Plus, it can't have been easy for him during those traumatic months. We decided to stay friends.

It was also important for me not to be so reliant on one person. He'd helped me so much, but now I needed to stretch my own wings and deal with any flare-ups on my own.

Where I had begun university feeling trapped in my own skin, now I had begun to heal.

Finally, with another new tool in my toolkit, I felt ready to emerge from my cocoon, to carve out a fresh start myself – one of strength and independence.

I was ready.

CHAPTER 3

Butterfly

Eczema has governed most of my decisions throughout my life. It's informed so many choices – from studying abroad to my interest in natural health. It's informed and continues to inform where I go, who I go with and what I do. But, rather than see that as a terrible drag, I've come to see that as a useful guide.

Not long ago, I saw my eczema as a bad thing. Now, I actually feel like I'm blessed because my eczema acts like a signal for when things aren't right. It literally signposts when I should consider spending time with a different circle of friends, or when I should live in a different environment. My body tells me, through my eczema, that something isn't working out, and then I use what I've learned over the years to guide me in the right direction. In this way eczema acts as a compass.

If it wasn't for my eczema, I wouldn't have made the choice to move abroad and go to California. And that was one of the happiest experiences of my entire life. I met such kind people, I found out that you don't need alcohol to have fun. And it really made me who I am today.

If it wasn't for my eczema, I wouldn't have learned the power of thought and how our reality is so often impacted by our positive (and negative) thinking.

I've now developed and grown into someone who has hope for a brighter future.

However, before I could fully emerge from my cocoon, I still needed to find the final pieces of the jigsaw which, once fitted together, would show me how to manage my eczema and stay on top of it from that day forward.

Only then would I fully emerge into the butterfly I had always dreamt of becoming and be able to spread my wings in the direction of the eczema-free life I longed to live.

back to work

University had finished, and so had my relationship with my boyfriend, but on good terms. After university I started working as a buyer for my dad, after looking for jobs all over. In fact, I applied for a chef assistant job at a raw food café in London, got offered a front of house position (since I hadn't enough chef experience), but backed out with the fear of moving to fast-paced London, working in my dream wellness industry and my eczema coming back.

I was worried my life would crumble again, so felt it was safer to live at home and work for my dad. And, although grateful for having this privilege, this also made me feel ashamed for relying on him once again.

It was exciting working on interior design projects for our homes, but although I thrived on the task of creating mood boards and meeting with architects, there was still something missing. I loved talking about the possibilities of creating crystal and aromatherapy-infused steam rooms with different spa companies, and I learned so much from the meetings my dad invited me to attend for his property company. Yet I still felt guilty for having to turn to my dad for a job, and still didn't feel like I was living the life I knew I was capable of creating for myself.

I still longed to run my own business, write a book and help people like me, but I felt trapped because of my lack of belief in my capabilities. It seems silly now, but after my eczema hospitalisation I lost all my self confidence in normal environments. However, just being in meetings without feeling anxious helped me to slowly rebuild my confidence, feel less anxious and more capable. I set up my own stall at Bygone Times – an antiques and collectables centre in Chorley – to sell my old clothes and earn some extra money, but I still had this burning desire to help others.

Meanwhile, I cherished the support of good friends to whom I'd begun to open up. For example, one friend, Giorgia, came up north at the end of university when my relationship ended to offer her support. She knew the change was going to be hard for me, and she literally held my hands if I reached to scratch my arms in bed that week and took me on daily adventures to keep me happy. So I added 'support' to my checklist of tools.

Appreciating the support of friends also made me miss those who were no longer here, such as my mentor, Polly Noble, who had lost her battle with cancer. I had been devastated when I found out and the news of her passing had amplified the uncertainty of life. I remember being at a petrol station when I heard the news. I drove out, but had to pull over because I was crying so hard and could barely breathe. Nobody really knew just how much of a positive impact Polly had on my life, but I hope she did.

As I reflected on our time together, it made my heart sink to think how I was juggling projects that weren't really me. I'd been on the right path with that internship, but I'd lost my way, and my confidence began to slip again. I was also missing my sister who was on her own solo world tour.

Before long my appetite reduced, my coffee consumption increased, and my restrictive eating resurfaced. Real meals seemed too huge for me, so I stopped eating them. I had unknowingly become lost again and, although I was controlling my eczema far better than I had done previously, my lack of purpose was having a significant effect on my wellbeing. Bewildered, I watched my skin flare up again.

london calling

Thankfully, I had some tools in my toolkit this time and my own checklist. I knew that environment, exercise and food were important, and that I needed to invest some time getting calm and more positive.

Instinctively, I was drawn back to the natural world which always set my soul on fire. So I enrolled myself on a course in making natural skincare products at CNM, something that would distract me from my growing anxiety and my fear of returning to that dark place where I'd been consumed by eczema. Perhaps that would give me a much-needed confidence boost? I knew too that in London I'd get the chance to rest my mind and eat well. So off I went.

After finishing the course, I returned to my hotel and booked myself a massage. But the beautician refused to massage me because my skin had become raw again. I burst into tears and felt a flash of fear run through me. I knew that I needed to de-stress and calm my mind if I wanted to calm my skin. But here I was again. My eczema was preventing me from having a calming massage, and as the panic began to rise, I asked her, with desperation in my voice, whether she thought I should go on a detox retreat and cut out certain foods.

Now that I know how the brain works I can see that my emotional brain was fully engaged, and as a result, I was in fight or flight mode and not letting in any logical information. The only way to think clearly in this emotional state is to get calm.

Thankfully the beauty therapist sat me down and suggested I do some yoga. I was grateful for her giving up her time to listen to me, and I took her advice. I needed to put myself first again because my stressed out mind was running the show and, when that happens, it can lead to terrible decision-making and result in poor choices. The only way to regain control was to fully relax. So I returned to my hotel with a natural moisturiser, a magnesium supplement and a mission to get calm.

I ordered room service of a green juice, some grilled salmon and vegetables, then had a surprise visit from my friend Joey. I'd told him not to come; that I 'wasn't well', but there he was in my room drinking peppermint tea, showing he cared about me. I slept like a baby that night. That's the healing power of support for you!

The next morning, I spoke to my sister, Rochelle, on the phone and ate a healthy breakfast. Then my childhood best friend Lamara turned up for dinner with me. I hadn't seen her in years, but she was here for me.

I remember feeling intensely loved and supported. And it dawned on me that this feeling was one of the missing jigsaw puzzle pieces. While I'd always had the support of my family, I'd been keeping my friends at arms' length during the worst of my eczema. But now they were making their presence felt and it made the world of difference. Slowly but surely, my eczema was healing.

The next day, I invested in some self-care with a blow dry and went shopping with some friends. I focused on feeding my soul. I now had a boyfriend I had known since childhood, and he arrived to tour London with me. We ate and slept well and I thought about the importance of other people in my healing journey.

That gave me an idea.

On my final night I asked my dad if I could meet my sister for her birthday in Australia. The prospect of such a treat on the horizon spurred me on and gave me something to look forward to.

I focused on my positive affirmations, saying 'I am well' over and over each night, and before long my eczema started to clear up. Looking back, I realise it was because not only did I feel supported and nourished by others and replenished by upping my self-care, I also had something to look forward to – a meaningful pursuit. That was a critical realisation. But it wasn't until much later that I'd realise how important that was. Little did I know then that this trip with my sister would give me the final puzzle pieces and provide the nourishing support and purposeful journey that I needed to fully emerge from my cocoon.

the wonderful magic of oz

For the whole month that I back-packed round Australia with my sister, I had zero eczema. The trip was a dream come true – not only was I in a warm climate, I was able to spend time with one of my favourite people on the planet and, together, we were on a purposeful journey with the aim of getting ourselves from one destination to another.

I'd always wanted to go to Australia. Even when I was 18, I'd asked if I could study at university there to chase a different and sunnier life. Now I was finally getting my wish.

The trip was incredibly freeing. As soon as I stepped off the plane in Sydney that evening, I felt like I might burst with excitement. I was due to catch a connecting flight in the morning to meet my sister in Melbourne, so I dropped my bags at the airport hotel and went straight to meet my high-school best friend Gemma who had recently moved out there. We drank red wine and chatted all evening, and I felt my soul filling up again. I was so happy.

Of course, you may be thinking, 'Wouldn't we all be happy if we had a whole month off from our responsibilities to trek across a warm country?'– and yes, I've been incredibly lucky. But, this experience has taught me, healing doesn't always require a grand gesture or a big action. No, I've learned that it's the small daily actions we can take in our everyday lives that can have the most impact.

For example, putting an event in the diary, something to look forward to, is a wonderful pick-me-up that can bring meaning into our lives. Committing to connect with a treasured friend for just five minutes each day can provide the mental boost and warmth that we each need. Connection is a soulful exchange for both parties, and if we can devote time to encourage more of that in our daily lives, we'll benefit.

I was on a big 'journey of a lifetime' adventure, but we can each plan mini-adventures or even micro-adventures very single month. And they needn't cost the earth. From solo trips to the cinema to paddle-boarding with friends; from horse-riding and nature-walking to tree-climbing, we can always choose activities that fill up our soul, even if they only take place at weekends.

The next morning before my flight I ate a full English breakfast. My appetite had returned. Not just for food, but for life!

Once I'd met my sister in Melbourne, we checked in to a luxury hotel as a treat for her birthday. After back-packing for many months, my sister appreciated a fresh shower, good food and a mooch around Melbourne before visiting Love Lock Bridge, where thousands of padlocks had been attached to the bridge as a sign of love for each other.

Once replenished by the luxurious surroundings, though, she was ready to jump back into the hostel life of meeting new people. So that's what we did.

We checked into a hostel with a bunch of other friendly English travellers. Ten of us shared a room and a bathroom, and it reminded me of being back at boarding school, which was strangely comforting. However, the drinking games began, so I took myself off for an early night. I was jet lagged anyway, but I also knew I needed to make the right choices for myself and my own wellbeing. Keeping check of my sleep and alcohol intake was critical for me to stay well on this trip.

The next morning, Rochelle was totally embarrassed by my insistence on doing sit-ups in the hostel room and doing squats on the side of the road as we waited for our buses. But I needed to be strict with myself in order to stay well, so that's what I did. If there's anything I've learned on this journey, it's that self-care means caring for yourself first. It means looking after your whole self – mind, body and soul – at every opportunity. Self-care is a choice we make over and over again every single day.

a healthy dose of inspiration

The next day I met up with an Australian friend I had met back in 2012. Sammi had flown all the way from Australia to be at this juicing event I was working at on the first day of my internship for a health company. It was the day after my 21ˢᵗ birthday, and she saw me well and happy to have started my internship. We were both buzzing at how passionate we both were about natural health and beauty – it was like meeting my Aussie soul sister. We stayed in touch ever since that day.

That internship may not have worked out as I'd hoped, but knowing I'd always have this connection made me see the silver lining and how, no matter how bad things get, there's always something to be grateful for. I was so grateful to reconnect with her again.

We talked about our shared passion for health and wellness, and she told me that she had created a business, was writing a book, and was now a qualified health coach. She was on the same path as me and was achieving her goals and living her true purpose. I felt so inspired – not only was she living her dream, she was living my dream too!

As we tucked in to a healthy Paleo breakfast, I quizzed her about her business and found my passion for starting my own business one day had been reignited. That's when I realised that spending time with like-minded souls who inspire and encourage you is such a vital part of living a good life. She kindly made lots of Paleo treats for us to take on our trip, and as I waved goodbye, I knew she had given me the impetus I needed to get back on track.

Next stop was Canberra, the capital of Australia, where my mum's side of the family live. After a scary 18-hour bus journey, during which the bus had broken down and we had all piled out onto the dusty road to wait for it to be fixed, we finally arrived.

I felt so at home. We were staying with my mum's cousin Gabby, who I already knew, but I was yet to meet my mum's uncle and the rest of the family. As they filtered one by one into the kitchen, it was like we'd known them all our lives. There is something so magical about connecting with long lost family members – the connection is strong despite having only seen them in photographs. After breakfast, Gabby would bundle us all into the car and take us to healthy cafés, or to visit an indigenous art museum, and we even went on Segways!

Next stop was Sydney where we stayed with our cousin Amy, a kindred spirit who is also into health and wellness and runs a yoga class every sunrise. I admired her courage to move to Australia to pursue her dreams and cherished the time we spent with her on Bondi Beach, at The Ivy and various other memorable places. I felt so at home here in the blissful warmth of the sunshine; I wanted to stay. I often sat with my knees pulled in to my chest, looking out to sea considering how that might be possible. But, as was the way with this trip, it was soon time to move on, and we were due to meet up with another cousin, Danny, in Brisbane.

Danny had also relocated to live in Australia and, like me, had suffered badly from eczema when he lived in England. Seeing him here in Australia so happy and clear-skinned gave me a boost, and reminded me how much our environment matters. He had done what was right for him and it was working. But, it was soon time to say goodbye as Byron Bay beckoned.

We stayed for one night, then took a trip on a Whitsundays boat tour for three days where we met two incredible American girls, Fran and Lila.

I was so inspired by Lila, as she lived with the condition spina bifida, yet was one of the most positive, confident girls I have ever met. She was like a ray of sunshine. The way she loved and rocked her body despite this condition gave me so much respect and admiration for her. I confided in her about my lifelong struggle with eczema, and she made me laugh and helped me see my own comparatively minor condition as so small and insignificant. Nothing would stop her achieving her dreams and living the life she was destined to lead, so nothing should stop me.

And achieve her dreams, she did. Lila is now a comedian in LA and has her own successful YouTube channel. Knowing the challenges she faces yet overcomes with optimism each day filled me with hope and pride. She taught me so much, for which I'll be eternally grateful.

Rochelle wanted to stay for an extra day, but I was ready to move on with our new friends Lila and Fran. So my incredibly independent sister said, 'Ok, bye then. I'll finish the trip myself'. I felt devastated as I thought we were parting, but Rochelle saw how I upset I was and begrudgingly threw her bags into their car and we left together. This was the only time we'd had a difference of opinion in the whole trip.

But the drama didn't end there. We arrived at the hostel on Magnetic Island in the middle of the night to discover the hostel was too full for Rochelle and I. As it had been my idea to move on, I felt responsible and panic set in. The hostel offered us a tent, but it was raining hard and the risk of a sleepless night and possibility of my eczema flaring up filled me with dread.

In desperation, I quickly called my boyfriend who managed to source an Airbnb and a taxi to get us there. It was such a relief and, having been apart for so long, I think my boyfriend enjoyed coming to our rescue. I was so grateful for his support –it made me realise that support can come from thousands of miles away, and made me appreciate that, even though she lives in New York City now, my strong and supportive relationship with my sister will never falter.

Our trip came to an end in Cannes. The month had flown by and I wasn't ready to leave. Yet, as the trip evolved, my sister and I realised how important our family and friends were to us, and I had missed my boyfriend terribly. This realisation made me see I couldn't return to live in Australia. It was just too far away from the people I loved so dearly.

Rochelle and I still speak every single day without fail. But, with each of us being on our own journey in life and living in different countries, it's rare to get so much consistent time together in each other's company.

So I shall always cherish this beautiful bonding experience we shared as we travelled across Australia together – two sisters adventuring across beautiful beaches, exploring cosmopolitan cities, travelling on the open road and taking in iconic wonders as we went.

The two of us are like chalk and cheese, yin and yang. She's a sociable extrovert with tonnes of energy who runs at a million miles per hour, whereas I'm an introvert who prefers peaceful evenings and a chilled night in. She's super organised and I'm more creative, which often leads to unorganised chaos. She's spontaneous and does things on the spur of the moment. I prefer to think things through and make calculated decisions.

We are so different, yet something special happens when we are together. We seem to balance each other out. Rochelle pulls me out of my shell and I calm her down. She encourages the adventurous side of me and I pull her into relax and 'listen to your body' mode. As such, we bring out the best in each other.

I feel blessed to be so close to my sister, even when we are far apart geographically. This trip made us fully appreciate our closeness and want to carve out a life where we live closer to one another one day. Until then, we knew we'd always have each other's backs, and that is such a comfort to know.

As I made my way to the airport, I began to feel worried about leaving my sister to settle back in the UK again. What if my eczema returned, like it had when I'd returned from California? What if I couldn't cope without the constant support of my sister? I could feel the spiral of negativity engulf me, so I started to fact-check, one of my strategies for dealing with anxiety.

I reminded myself that I had plenty of other support now that I had opened up about my condition and was far better equipped to deal with any flare-ups if they arose than I'd ever been before. My support circle may stretch across all corners of the globe, but it still exists and that is enough for me.

I reflected on the trip and the puzzle pieces that had fitted together as I waited in the line at passport control:

- I had slept like a baby, used natural products on my skin, and spent time surrounded by supportive kind people.

- I had moved my body each day in a way that it loved, and the adventure of getting from A to B had given me a sense of purpose.
- I'd been reading a mindfulness book, so had been practising living in the moment and savouring each experience by soaking each one of those moments up.
- I'd benefited from a whole month of ecotherapy from being outdoors in the fresh air, exploring the wilds and the cities of Oz.
- I'd used positive affirmations on long bus journeys, such as 'I can do this,' 'I'm living my best life,' and 'I am free'.

The result was tremendous. I had no eczema but, most of all, I had hope for a brighter future.

the missing puzzle piece

I felt rejuvenated, but there was something else. Something which had shifted inside me – a clarity around what I was meant to do in my life – a clearer sense of purpose. Meeting like-minded kindred spirits on this trip had motivated me to pursue my own dream of serving others with eczema. It was then that the final jigsaw piece slotted into place – the missing piece was PURPOSE!

As I stepped onto the plane, rather than feeling dread about returning to the colder climate, I was excited to see my boyfriend again. I was excited about something else too. Not just excited, I was positively buzzing! I spent the next 24 hours travelling home wide-awake, writing my business plan about what I would offer the world. I had learned so much during my battle with eczema and plenty more on this trip, and I was determined to share what I'd learned with others, no matter what it took.

I remembered all the times I'd opened my laptop, desperate to find something; someone who could help give me hope that my eczema could be managed. But all I found was people complaining about how bad it was, with no real solutions or positive experiences at all. I remember not wanting to approach it in an emotional way, because I didn't want to pull myself even lower. I wanted someone to tell me I was going to come out of it. And I couldn't find anyone.

I remember that was when I had first thought: 'I'm going to be that person, I'm going to pull myself out of it, and then I'm going to pull other people out of it too, and show that there is a way.' That purpose had lain dormant within me until now. For now was the time to make this happen, to be that person for others.

My confidence had returned because I had back-packed for a whole month, staying in new and different locations, and my skin was glowing! As the plane touched down in the UK, I gripped my business plan firmly in my hand, resolute that I would do whatever I needed to bring this plan to fruition and make it happen within the next year.

I'd been awake for 48 hours straight, but I had never had a clearer plan for my future. I'd woken up to the possibilities, and stepping off that plane felt like the first stage of emerging from my life-long cocoon into the realms of possibility and a purposeful life.

Before I'd gone away, I'd been wondering why eczema had still flared up despite being equipped with the tools I'd gathered. I'd been eating and exercising well, sleeping well, and I'd been using NLP techniques such as positive affirmation to calm my mind when stress bubbled up. But still I'd had that flare-up which had prevented me from having a massage.

But then, it dawned on me, it was only when the two final missing pieces of the healing jigsaw puzzle had come together – SUPPORT and PURPOSE – that I had fully healed. Of course, I still get the occasional flare-up, but they are so very rare now. And I'm able to nip it in the bud almost immediately – making me as eczema-free as I'll ever be.

While I'd been working for my dad, although I enjoyed the work, my lack of purpose had been causing me concern. At the back of my mind I'd been feeling like I wasn't fulfilling my true potential as I wasn't pursuing natural health in my career, nor was I doing anything to help other people who suffered from this condition. While my support had grown and shown itself as one of the missing pieces, purpose was the final missing piece of the puzzle.

With a great sense of pride and fulfilment, I added 'Purpose' with a capital 'P' to my checklist. I had a new mission, an aim to save enough money to pay for my own training to start my wellness business. So that is exactly what I did.

I was back home in Manchester working for my dad again, but this time it was different. This time it was the means to an end; my work had a purpose. By working I could earn enough money to invest in my dream career. This time I was eating well, saving money and dreaming about my future business, and I was in regular contact with my support network. I was ticking all the boxes, and now I had the missing piece. Having this drive and sense of purpose – something to work towards; something to contribute to the world – was powerful. It calmed my mind. So I got my head down and worked hard so I could save up to fund my own dream.

I thought about my business every single day. I'd write Post-it notes about everything I wanted to achieve and share with the world, and stick them onto my laptop screen, or on my fridge at home, anywhere I regularly looked. I would tell myself each morning when I woke and each evening before I slept exactly what I was aiming for and I'd share my dreams with friends.

I affirmed "I am a successful entrepreneur", "I have a successful website", "I am the healthiest and happiest I have ever been". I read books like *Think and Grow Rich*, listened to Tony Robbins audio tapes and watched the Wayne Dyer movie. I also checked in with Louise Hays' book *You Can Heal Your Life*, making notes to keep me positive. Anything to keep me motivated.

I created a vision board with a section on saving money, a section on becoming an entrepreneur, and a section each on health, love and family. Then I glued on images of a beach lifestyle where I could work from anywhere. I put whatever mattered most to me on that vision board.

It didn't matter to me how silly people might think my ideas were – I wasn't going to give up on my vision.

Equally, I wasn't going to give up on my self-care either. I used the Headspace app to practice mindfulness, I went to the gym every day, did daily runs, spent time cooking healthy meals and went on daily morning nature walks with my mum. I relaxed and explored healthy cafés with my boyfriend at weekends and travelled to see my siblings in London whenever I could. I mindfully ate all my meals, being thankful for them for nourishing my body. I also took as many trips abroad to the sunshine as I could.

pursuing the dream

One year later, in June 2016, I took the first concrete step towards pursuing my true purpose in life. Finally, it was time to invest in myself; to stand on my own two feet. I spent all of the savings I'd earned on a health coaching course with IIN (Institute of Integrative Nutrition). By taking that action to train to become a health coach, I set the wheels in motion towards my dream. It was the start of something that set my heart back on fire, as I was finally doing something for me – something that I knew 100 per cent I really wanted to do.

I almost didn't sign up, though. I started to fret about whether the investment would be worth it. Would I be a good enough health coach? That internal radio station in my head, that criticises and questions my actions started playing – so much so that I left it until a few hours before enrolment was about to end, before I called up and put my deposit for the course down.

I took a deep breath and reminded myself that this was one step in the direction of creating my dream life. I just had to follow my strong gut feeling and take action. It helped that the course was online, so I didn't feel trapped by location and could do the work whenever I found time. It was the best decision I've ever made.

Another reason I picked that course was that it wasn't all about nutrition, but also focused on some of the other topics which featured on my own health and wellness checklist, such as environment, career and relationships. So it just made sense. The course clarified the notes I'd scribbled down on a piece of paper all those years ago, and following my heart in this way gave me a sense of pride and joy that I'd never felt before.

I noticed this sense of true direction was a powerful way to respond to my inner critic and that committee that we all have telling us we can't, shouldn't, won't be good enough/ able to, and so on. Pursuit of purpose is a great way to help silence that committee, and instead rallies your cheerleading committee to support you in your endeavours, which is very handy indeed.

That said, you still need a support network to bolster your own belief in yourself. All of the puzzle pieces need to fit together in order to truly thrive. For me this was the final piece of the puzzle.

Once I'd made the decision to do the course I became so excited, I couldn't wait to get stuck in. The course started a month later and, once it did, every evening and weekend I'd watch lectures and take the weekly exams.

As soon as my dad heard about me investing in the course, he could see what lengths I had gone to in order to follow my passion. One day he walked in on me doing a practice consultation and, thinking I was Skyping a friend, he waved and said 'hello'. It was time to tell him what I was doing.

He pulled me into his office and asked me what I truly wanted to do with my life. At first I was scared to tell him my plans, fearful that he might think it sounded too 'pie in the sky'. I wanted to be like my other siblings, involved in the family business and passionate about property. However, I couldn't hold it in and I burst into tears, something I rarely do as I don't like to cry in front of my dad.

I explained how my eczema had taken over my life, how I'd tried everything, and how I wanted to qualify as a health coach and write a book to help everyone suffering all over the world. I was worried about what he might think of me, but he passed me tissues whilst listening intently. Needless to say, I left his office with his full support to pursue my dream, which was a huge moment for me.

I'd proven to my dad how much I wanted it by investing my own time and money in it. I hadn't relied on his support; I'd just gone out there and done it. That impressed him and was a big deal for him, and for me.

I still worked for my dad, but he granted me the time during the day to study on my course whenever I had finished what needed doing for him. My commitments for him grew less as my health coaching studying took priority. I was finally pursuing my dream, and I was so happy.

What was wonderful was that the initial action of deciding with intention to purposefully serve others by qualifying as a health coach had led to the first step, but that provided the catalyst to changing my life and led to the second step, which was to add another string to my health and wellness bow.

In the last month of my health coaching diploma, one year after I'd lit the spark to fuel my passion in a career in health, I invested in a natural chef diploma course. I would soon qualify as a health coach, and now I would travel to my natural chef class in London, run through the nutrition slides of what we were about to cook, then spend the afternoon cooking and taste-testing the foods. We'd then go home with assignments to re-create our own version of the dish, write up the recipe and health benefits, and do additional reading and prep for the following class.

It was so exciting and nourishing for me to spend my time learning about nutrition and creating nutritional dishes while I finished my health coaching course in the evenings.

The natural chef course included a whole range of dietary cooking: from vegan, paleo, and gluten-free to raw foods, healthy baking, and so on. We learned all the therapeutic values of the foods and about which foods are good for which ailments. We were taught how to write a therapeutic food plan and how to cost up and write up recipes. We learned how to budget buy when cooking a range of dishes in class, and found out about the various business ventures open to us after qualifying.

Each day was different, and I cherished the variety. One day we'd study knife techniques, fermentation and sprouting and the next day we'd learn about raw foods, soups, spices and healthy baking. There'd be a daily practice of skills, nutritional lecture slides to run through and assignments to write up. I was in my element.

It made me feel so proud of myself for pursuing another passion of mine! Without anyone's advice, I had jumped into another dream course. I finally felt like I had my own back. I realised that, as well as having the support of my dear friends and family, I finally had the support of myself. I was on a mission to educate myself as much as possible to pursue my dream business.

Kris, the manager who had invited me to finish my internship with him, stayed in touch and I introduced him to my raw chocolate making friend. They ran a few retreats abroad, and he asked if I would like to work as a chef for his retreats when I finished my diploma. The opportunities were opening up, and I was finally emerging from my cocoon.

qualified butterfly ~ living the dream

In August 2017 I graduated as a qualified health coach and began to work on my website, my social media and my book – this book. And yes, this does make me squeal with excitement at regular intervals.

On the day I graduated as a health coach, I was at the airport, about to fly off to see my best friend in Canada. I'd got so stuck in to my new chef course, I'd hardly given myself the time to fully take in and appreciate what I had completed. But here I was staring at my phone, for I was finally qualified. I could officially call myself a health coach! I received an e-mail with my certificate as I was about to go through airport security, and instantly felt a huge sense of pride. I had done it!

My mum sent me a congratulations card, and I decided to dedicate my Canada trip to celebrating this wonderful achievement. It was the first qualification that felt so right for me. That leap of faith I took investing in the course had totally paid off, and still makes me feel incredibly happy. It was made all the more delightful because of what I had been through. My intense journey made me appreciate it all the more.

serving others

Now that vision that I'd had after leaving hospital has come to fruition, it feels like I am finally on track, and I still have to pinch myself daily. I sit in meetings and smile to myself that, with hard work and dedication, I've managed to make my dream a reality and made what seemed impossible, possible. Every day is so exciting!

One by one I began to attract coaching clients via my Instagram account. This was it! I could finally share what I had learned with others who were going through the same as I had. At first I was nervous sharing my story, and doubted my ability to help others. However, once I threw myself out there, clients reached out to get help gaining control over their skin, to gain more energy, sleep better, eat a healthier diet and live the life they deserve to live.

I shared the photos of me at my worst to demonstrate there's no shame in this condition, and to offer that sense of there being a light at the end of the tunnel – the light that I had struggled for so long to find.

I'm so proud of how far I've come. After the eczema event in 2013 that totally destroyed my soul, I've come such a long way. After being hospitalised, I withdrew and became very shy. I had no confidence in my abilities. I now have the confidence to go into any room with any person and tell them what I want to achieve in this world. I am no longer embarrassed about what happened to me, but proud I managed to overcome it.

That strength is something that no job with a high wage could have given me. For someone who wanted to shy away from the world and almost disappear, I am proud for throwing myself into the deep end and refusing to give up on my dreams.

The first step to healing is letting out how you feel inside. So I cultivate space for my clients to do just that. For some, the solution is easier than they think. For example, one girl had terrible eczema but seemed to have all the pieces of the puzzle in place. She wasn't stressed, had a supportive network, loved her job and exercised and slept well. It was just her diet that was out of whack. So as soon as I substituted certain foods with other foods, within ten days her eczema had cleared up. She had been living with it for the past 15 years! She was as over the moon to find a solution as I was to have helped guide her towards it.

For many clients it's not just about their skin, it's about feeling better in their own skin. So goals we set together need to reflect that. Whether we find ways to boost confidence or live more purposefully, we focus on taking small steps, which provide a catalyst towards bigger changes.

Now I get such a buzz from helping people transform their lives. I've successfully coached clients and have received the most amazing feedback from them. They've told me I've helped them to build their confidence, understand their eczema triggers and replace despair with hope. That makes my entire journey worthwhile. That I've been able to make a real impact in the life of other eczema sufferers makes the most difficult times worth it.

I cried tears of joy the other day because a girl I'd coached emailed me to say that I'd changed her life, that she never thought it would be possible, and to thank me for making her excited about living. Her message of gratitude brought me exactly back to that moment when I was covered in eczema and decided that one day I would love to help others to heal. But I had to heal myself first.

The icing on the cake is that, now that I have this purpose and am ticking all of the boxes on my checklist, I rarely get any eczema at all. It only flares up when I feel under pressure, but now I know how to gain control and manage it.

The fact that I tried everything and nothing was working for me demonstrates to my clients that I know what they are going through. Thankfully I found that light at the end of the tunnel and am now in a position to share that light with the rest of the world.

That's why I've written this book and created so much free video and blog content on my website. I wanted to reach a wider audience than I could reach via my coaching practice; to make my journey and methods accessible to all, to anyone with an internet connection across the world – not just local people who could afford to be coached.

I'm developing the business in other ways too. My own natural moisturiser is in development and I'm planning to run some webinars, along with an online program and possibly retreats in the future too.

Now that I'm a health coach, natural chef and author, I'm able to share my passion for health and wellness far and wide. And I'm thankful for the journey I've been on.

the beauty of eczema

When you suffer from any condition, it can be exhausting; mentally draining. Sufferers can swing from feeling isolated to infuriated. But, as anyone who has ever suffered from any kind of adversity knows, it can also provide you with the gift of empathy and compassion for others. When you've endured something yourself, you are able to feel empathy for others who are going through it too.

Essentially, your condition can act as a springboard towards saving people from suffering. If you can use all that you've been through to help save others from going through the same, it will have been worth it. So, although I wish I didn't have eczema, I would never have this degree of empathy towards other people had I not experienced having eczema.

As such, there is a beauty in eczema, a beauty in suffering and a beauty in adversity. They can lead to lessons that you'd never had learned had you not been through that pain.

I've grown because of my eczema, not despite it. It's made me such a better person, it makes me not take life for granted. It's made me realise that who you are is far more important than what you look like; that your contribution is far more crucial than your appearance, and that perfect isn't attainable. In fact, striving for perfection can be soul-destroying. We are all good enough. Perfection gets in the way of that realisation and burdens us with impossible expectations to live up to.

Had I not been on this journey, I wouldn't have learned all of these incredibly valuable life lessons. I needed to go through it all to learn it all.

This whole experience has woken me up to this knowledge that nothing is perfect, and that what one person perceives as beautiful is different to what someone else may find beautiful. It's all a matter of perception. Showing up imperfectly is better than not showing up at all. And so that's what I strive to do now. Rather than strive for perfection, I strive to show up. No matter how imperfectly that may be.

Now that I've found a life beyond eczema, helping others to do the same is all that I want to do. After decades battling eczema, I'm so grateful that now I get to do just that.

And now you've read my story. The rest of this book is set out to equip everyone who reads it with the tools required to tick all of those important boxes and gain control over their skin.

I reveal my HOPE Principles, where you'll learn how important your home environment is to your wellness, how to cultivate an optimistic outlook and live a purposeful life. You'll learn why self-care is health-care, and how to pamper yourself with the right skin products and discover the importance of exercise, eating well and the all-important ecotherapy. You'll also learn why equipping yourself with tools to manage stress and surrounding yourself with supportive relationships is so important, and how the science of positive psychology can help you to not just survive eczema but to thrive in your life.

In the meantime, here are a few lessons I learned on my travels.

How To Nourish Yourself (Without Backpacking Round Australia)

- Carve out time to spend with like-minded souls who inspire and encourage you. Sign up to evening classes and you'll find people who are interested in the same things as you.
- Plan mini-adventures – give yourself something to look forward to.
- Have a purposeful destination and spend time taking steps towards it.
- Connect with family – near and far. Write letters, arrange visits, post gifts.
- Don't be afraid to ask for help. People who love you are always willing to offer guidance.

- Prioritise self-care. Not just pampering and treats, but taking care of your mind, body and soul. Have a self-care calendar where you add stars to show you've taken care of yourself that day.
- Seek out inspiration from people, books and films.
- Work towards a purpose. Save up what you earn from your job to invest in something you've always wanted to do.

Part 2: Stress, Support & HOPE

"Your body hears
everything your
mind says."

NAOMI JUDD

CHAPTER 4

Stress

For eczema sufferers, it's not only itching that keeps us up at night – stress does too. In fact, stress is one of the key causes behind eczema flare-ups. And that's important to be aware of because, I've found, managing eczema isn't so much about clearing up your skin. It's about figuring out WHY your skin is flaring up in the first place, and addressing that.

It's not about applying a miracle cream (even though moisturising really helps); it's about applying strategies and interventions to reduce stress and increase support. It's about making choices and changes where necessary.

Creams can reduce and manage eczema over the short term, but it's so vital to know what needs attending to as a longer-term solution. Perhaps you need more sleep or exercise? Perhaps you need to slow down and pause more often? Perhaps you need to connect with friends more, or work on changing your diet? Usually, though – almost always, I've found – you need to reduce the stress in your life or, if that's not possible, equip yourself with tools with which to deal with it and gain some respite from it.

Because stress has a lot to answer for.

According to research from the American Psychological Association, the majority of GP visits are stress-related, and $42 billion is spent annually on treating stress-related anxiety disorders in the USA. No wonder it prevents millions of people across the world from going to work, and so affects the productivity of entire nations. A similar story is playing out across the developed world as studies reveal we are living in an increasingly stressed-out society – and one in which stress isn't managed particularly well.

The bad news is, because the mind and the body are so closely connected, stress can cause a wide range of physical symptoms. The good news is that not all of these are negative, and there are strategies we can put in place to deal more effectively with stress.

Unfortunately, stress can adversely affect your skin, by affecting your gut flora which represents 70% of your immune system. Stress can also suppress or increase appetite, depending on how much cortisol is released. I've experienced times when I've lost my appetite due to stress and (like most people) have also experienced the comfort-eating side of stress.

Similarly, stress can make you feel tired and prevent sleep. The accelerated breathing and heart rate caused by stress can make you feel exhausted, but it can also prevent good sleep hygiene as the brain works hard to find solutions to worries, which adds to the exhaustion – and so it goes on. I don't know about you, but the more tired I am, the more likely I am to over-react to stressful experiences. And the more tired I am, the more likely I am to over-think things, which leads to eczema.

Furthermore, the more extreme types of stress are the number one predictor of depression and a whole bunch of chronic diseases. Stress can make us more likely to get poorly and stay poorly because when cortisol is released into our bloodstream, DHEA, a hormone which supports our immune system, cannot be released at the same time. Studies show that this means stressed-out people tend to catch more colds and find it difficult to shake them.

As well as our physical wellbeing, stress can adversely affect our mood in a way that feels uncontrollable. This is because everything seems more intense when we're stressed, caused by our nervous system becoming hyper-responsive, and our sensory receptors and sensitivity heightening, along with the amount of pressure we feel ourselves buckling under. As a result of this alarming pressure increase, we tend to react irrationally rather than responding calmly because our rational thinking skills are impaired when we're stressed.

Yes, if left untreated, stress can be a threat to both our physical and mental health.

But – and this is vital – it's important to remember that all of this is only true for **long-lasting stress.** Like anxiety, it is the *duration* which matters, and that's why stress is only dangerous if we ignore it and leave it untreated.

types of stress ~ harmful or harmless?

There are three types of stress – acute stress, episodic acute stress and chronic stress.

1. Acute stress is short-term and can be exhilarating in small doses. It can give us an energy boost to drive us to deliver to deadline or get through an exam. It's enough to cause a low level of emotional distress, such as irritability or anxiety, and can cause headaches and other aches and pains, but it is highly treatable and straightforward to manage. Our stress response is natural, but is only meant to be switched on for brief periods.

    In small doses, when turned on very briefly, the surge of stress hormones and quickened heart beat can actually enhance physical performance, making us more alert, faster and stronger, ready to face the perceived 'danger' our body is responding to – but only if it that fight or flight mode is quickly switched off soon afterwards.

2. Episodic acute stress applies to those who are unable to switch off these acute stressful moments and seem to be in a perpetual state of acute stress, finding themselves rushing from one stressful situation to the next, feeling overwhelmed and chaotic. This can lead to a constant feeling of worrying 'what if', and more persistent physical symptoms such as migraines, chest pain and hypertension.

    This kind of extreme ongoing stress requires prompt management. It's treatable, but sometimes medical help is advised if the person under this more long-lasting stress can't manage it appropriately. When high stress levels continue for a long period and get in the way of us living our daily lives, that's when medical help should be sought to help with lifestyle or behavioural changes or other solutions.

3. Chronic stress is altogether different. Chronic stress, like severe depression and anxiety, can cause those experiencing it to disengage from life. Chronic stress tends to occur when we ignore or fail to manage everyday stressors over a very long period of time or in response to trauma. This kind of stress is even more exhausting because it wears you down and can make you feel like there's no way out. It depletes the body's mental and physical resources that would ordinarily be able to help manage it, and is less easy to treat. This type of stress always requires some kind of medical and/or psychological intervention.

It's no wonder that episodic acute stress and chronic stress are so exhausting, as those experiencing either types have their physiological fight or flight response constantly switched to 'on', meaning blood pressure and heart rate are constantly higher. That's not a healthy state to be in. Partly because it's not good for the body or mind –but also because it can lead to the sufferer seeking ways to numb or distract them from the stress, such as smoking, drinking or other unhealthy coping mechanisms, which simply exacerbate the negative implications even further.

Evidently, it's only when the natural, everyday acute stress, which we all experience to varying degrees, becomes episodic or chronic stress that the damage can be done.

Conversely, small amounts of daily acute stress as a result of forgetting to do something we were meant to do, being late, being asked to deliver a document with a deadline of ten minutes ago– all of that is relatively normal and potentially manageable. And, the good news is, even small steps can help to significantly reduce acute stress, whether that's going for a daily walk or practising mindful breathing. More on the solutions to stress in a moment.

Before exploring the best tried and tested ways to effectively manage stress, it's important to understand the causes and signs of stress and, just as critical, to understand that, just as they are manageable, small doses of stress can even be helpful.

good stress: the silver lining

In fact, stress is a natural part of life, something none of us are immune from. It's part of what it means to be human. Just as feeling sad is part of the whole spectrum of human emotion, best accepted and felt rather than feared and ignored, so too is stress part of the human experience.

Like anything in life – too much is bad and a little might be good.

But even more critical to remember is that our stress response is actually there to help us survive, rather than harm us. It has a purpose. In this way, perhaps, rather than seeing stress as the enemy, we should see it as useful. That may sound crazy and contradictory considering how I've just spelled out how detrimental stress can be for mind, body and the GDP of entire nations! However, let me explain...

Stress has a purpose.

- Our stress response triggers our natural in-built fight or flight response. It puts us on high alert to fight or flee, which is useful in speeding up our reaction time, energising and motivating us to take action. According to the University of California, this can improve our physical performance (even if our cognitive performance tends to be marred by our emotional brain taking over from our logical limbic system).

- It acts as a hard-wired early warning system that something isn't quite right; a signal to do something differently, to tackle whatever our stress response is perceiving as dangerous. It alerts us to the fact that it is time to make some kind of change. For example: to slow down; to say 'no' to taking on more work; to look for a new job, new friendship group or new area to live in. As such, stress should be seen as an opportunity rather than a threat; as an opportunity to make the required changes, to learn new habits and to equip ourselves with tools that will help us to cope. Just as pain and disease signal the need for rest and recuperation, stress signals the same, along with the need to seek ways to shift habits or change our lifestyle or working environment to better serve us.

- It primes us to seek support. When stressed we release oxytocin via the pituitary gland. Oxytocin is often called the 'cuddle hormone' because it is also released when we hug. In this way, when we are stressed, our brain is literally encouraging us to seek support from others.

- It reminds us of our resilience. It is by getting through stressful experiences that we learn resilience, determination, optimism and how to self-soothe when the going gets tough.

Stressful experiences often yield valuable insight. If they are within our control to prevent, we can prevent them; if they are not within our control, it makes sense to accept that which we can't control and be comforted in the knowledge that there will likely be a valuable lesson in the experience, which will come in useful either now or sometime in the future. When we view stressful experiences in this way, we can see that even stress can be meaningful as a teacher.

Few people never ever get stressed. So it makes sense to view stress through the lens of opportunity rather than threat. Only those who have learned how to calm themselves have minimal stress in their lives. Of course, some people are more susceptible to stress than others – people working in high stress environments, such as stock market traders, hence the high burn-out rate. However, even the most stressed-out stock market trader can learn to manage stress, to tap into its motivational side and work through it to minimise its negative implications.

why do we get so stressed?

What I have learnt on my journey is that different things stress out different people. My triggers are different to your triggers, so it's important to get a good awareness and understanding around what causes you personally to feel stressed. Being clear on WHY you get stressed is as important as learning how to reduce stress. The WHY is almost always as important as the HOW.

For me, the key stressors and the most stressful periods of my life correlated with my eczema worsening. The converse is also true – the times I felt most happy and satisfied with all areas of my life resulted in my eczema disappearing.

For example, when I returned to England from Israel and was told I was no longer wanted for my internship, my eczema returned with a vengeance. The stress of commuting coupled with the isolation of living away from friends and family led to my hospitalisation, while securing enjoyable work and belief from people I respected helped reduce my eczema. The knock-on effect of this realisation has been a daily devotion to investing in my self-care, which has led to even less eczema.

signs of stress

If you know what to look for, if you increase your self-awareness about what it feels like in your body to feel stress, you can use your internal signals to know when you need to intervene and take action, to turn down the volume on your stress levels.

So, if you're feeling especially tearful, tired, or irritable or notice you're eating too much or too little, your body could be informing you that you are feeling stressed. If you are grinding your teeth at night, or experiencing tension headaches on either side of your head or have a tense neck and shoulders, your body could be informing you that you are feeling stressed. You then have a choice. You can ignore the signals and carry on as usual, or you can do something to relieve your stress. The former is not advisable given the effect of long-lasting or chronic stress. The latter is the preferable – and, indeed, only – option if you want to live a good and healthy life.

common causes

All kinds of stuff can cause stress. Triggers can be rooted in social, health, work, financial or lifestyle issues. It's always worth uncovering what tends to trigger your own stress, because self-awareness is the first step towards stress-management (and 'self-management', which includes self-compassion, self-care and self-soothing).

Sometimes we don't instantly realise what is causing us stress. During my coaching practice, I've found people often perceive they have a problem in one area, but it's actually coming from a problem in another area of their lives. For example, the emotional eater who hates their career, or the person who thinks they're exhausted because of the stress of their work, but are actually mentally drained as a result of not having any supportive friends to share their life with.

As you read through the HOPE Principles in the second half of this book, you'll be able to notice which areas you are lacking or are causing you stress or worry. Often, stress comes from pressure. So, in the interests of getting to know yourself and what fires up your fight or flight stress response, let's explore some of the more common causes of the pressure which leads to stress.

According to the NHS, stress is defined as "the feeling of being under too much mental or emotional pressure". The contributors to that pressure can vary.

Overwhelm

When the number of tasks on your to-do list or the sheer scale of a challenge ahead of you seems insurmountable. When you have been juggling too much for too long and it all just gets too much! In this situation it's important to hit the pause button and reset. We'll explore ways to do that in this chapter, and in the HOPE Principles section of this book.

Expectations

Living up to expectations (others or your own). This is a big one. I spend a lot of time worrying if I'm good enough – am I a good enough daughter, sister, adviser, friend? Will my YouTube videos be good enough to inspire and help other people in my situation? The stories we tell ourselves about not being good enough and the questioning of our capabilities all stem from our inner critic.

Often our beliefs are inaccurate and have either come from other people or from our own repetition of negative judgements that are not based on fact, but are based on our own insecurities. The way to tackle this kind of pressure is to fact-check and re-frame, which we'll explore at the end of this chapter.

Change

Change can be stressful. Taking on new responsibilities, such as a new job, house or baby, along with the uncertainty around what might happen as a result of this change can cause stressful feelings. What if we can't do what we need to do in order to make this change work? These future-based worries can feed our anxiety around change. And the uncertainty around change simply magnifies it.

Our what-ifs tend to come from future-based anxious thoughts, but we cannot predict or know the future. Rather than wonder or worry about what might happen, it makes far more sense to focus on what is happening now – which is where mindfulness comes in (more on that later).

Perfectionism

The pressure to exceed expectations and do things perfectly is huge. I am a natural perfectionist, and in the past I mentally beat myself up if I wasn't achieving as much as I felt I should be. Even when trying to get my eczema under control, I would eat what I thought was the 'perfect' diet, but mentally I was totally over-whelmed and stressed with my lifestyle. I wasn't aware that this was one of the biggest elements I needed to get under control for my 'healing'. Being good enough is enough.

de-stressing solutions

There are many changes we can make to our lifestyle that support stress reduction, such as eating more healthily, exercising more frequently, getting adequate sleep, nurturing our relationships, and practising mindfulness. These are vastly better for us than the sedentary and unhealthy numbing strategies we tend to use to distract us, like drinking alcohol, over-eating or scrolling through social media.

We numb ourselves rather than nourish ourselves because it feels easier. But these unhealthy methods of avoidance, denial and distraction don't get rid of the stress – they just numb and blur it, but it's still there bubbling under the surface. When we choose to nourish ourselves instead and opt for interventions that have been proven to reduce stress, we choose life and make steps towards minimising stress in our lives.

There are things we can do after a stressful day, but there are also things we can do in the moment of impact – during stressful experiences to help lower the stress levels in real time. Some of these are cognitive and involve noticing a situation or reaction and reframing it, using our thinking brain.

The other solutions are more about sensation, awareness and embodiment, and don't involve thinking. Because of the way our brain works (our thinking brain isn't reachable when our emotional brain is engaged), it makes sense to use the strategies that DON'T involve thinking first.

In fact, it's difficult for us humans to even be able to pause and use the rational part of our brain until we've deployed the strategies which use our body rather than our brain first; the ones that calm our body, soothe our senses and regulate our stress response. Then we are able to view what's happening with clarity, and respond wisely.

Breathe

When we breathe big deep breaths in and out, we enter the 'rest and digest' mode rather than the 'fight or flight' mode. This is because we activate the body's parasympathetic nervous system. Slow deep rhythmic belly breathing (diaphragmatic breathing) stimulates our relaxation response. This type of breathing is in contrast to the fast, shallow chest breathing that we do when we're stressed. To deepen the relaxation, you can extend the exhale by an extra couple of counts. For instance, you could breathe in for four, hold for two, and then breathe out for six.

Repeat deep breathing exercises three times – so in for four and out for six, three times – and you'll feel calmer and more able to respond in a measured way.

Breathing is something we do naturally in order to stay alive, but it's something we can do purposefully in order to thrive, because it literally counters the stress response of the body –which means our heart doesn't have to work as hard.

Count

Counting can be a useful way to distract you and focus your cognitive mind on something else.

Next time you're stressed, try counting the number of red cars you can see nearby or count backwards from 100 in sevens. That will temporarily take your mind off the stressor.

Move and align your body

It's widely reported that exercise improves mood, but it can also improve memory too, as stress shrinks the hippocampus, which is the area of the brain responsible for memory. What's more, when we raise our heart rate we can even reverse damage caused by long-term stress or traumatic events, and the neuro-hormones released when we move our bodies can improve our cognitive function and make us more open to learning.

Meanwhile, posture is also important. When we spend a few minutes checking and correcting our posture to make sure we are aligned and noticing any areas of tension so we can relax those muscles, we can literally lift our mood and prime ourselves to deal with any stress. So a change of pace, scenery and posture can positively change our state of mind.

Remember, our system and our responses were designed to protect our ancestors from danger lurking round the corner. If our ancestors stopped to reframe or use any of the stress-reduction strategies that use thinking, the sabre-tooth tiger would have snapped them up before they could say 'cognitive reappraisal'. The fight or flight response put them on high alert so they could respond quickly to the danger. During that response it's difficult to think straight, so only by using one of the bodily strategies to reduce stress could they then calm themselves and think with greater clarity.

These days stressors don't tend to be as life-threatening as the dreaded sabre-tooth. A looming deadline or concern about stepping up on stage won't kill us, but our brain and body reacts to those stressful situations as if they were as dangerous as the aforementioned tiger.

The key point to remember is that our brain and body is wired to do this unconsciously. It's our auto-pilot response, but it's not the response we might choose if we were able to think clearly about the situation. That's why learning methods to calm ourselves down is so crucial to managing everyday stress.

Cry

Having a good cry is good for you. Tears have an important function, kind of like a safety valve for overtly stressful situations, because when you cry, excess cortisol (the stress hormone) is released in your tears. This hormonal release explains why we tend to feel much better after a good cry.

Take prebiotics and probiotics

We need both to enable good mental and physical health. Probiotics are the living good bacteria which cultivate good gut health, and prebiotics are the non-living food for those probiotics which nourish them. Research published in the Frontiers in Behavioural Neuroscience journal shows that a regular intake of prebiotics can protect against the effects of stress, and restore healthy sleep patterns after a stressful situation.

Probiotics are found in cultured or fermented foods such as yoghurt, sauerkraut, miso and kombucha. Prebiotics are found in legumes, asparagus, chicory, onions, leeks, oats, garlic, and Jerusalem artichokes. We'll explore more about eating well to manage eczema in the E part of the HOPE Principles.

Reframe

This is otherwise known as cognitive reappraisal or self-directed neuroplasticity, and it's the practice of cultivating more optimistic thinking and more accurate and useful beliefs by considering different ways of looking at things. It's important to do sometimes, because it's quite natural for us humans to fall into a variety of thinking traps where we jump to conclusions and worry about worst-case-scenarios – despite the evidence often proving otherwise. When we feel stressed, it's our emotional memories that are encoded, not factual ones, so we need to be able to reframe what isn't true.

The thing is – it's near-impossible to stop thinking about something. It's what scientists call our 'attention bias', which is often focused on the negative in order to protect us from those no-longer-existent sabre-tooth tigers. So the only way to get rid of negative thoughts is to replace them. For example, if I said to you 'don't think about a purple penguin', you'd think about a purple penguin.

Of course, you can distract yourself, but the thought will soon resurface – so it's better to work with the thought. If the thought motivates you to work harder, it is serving you – but if it makes you stressed and anxious without spurring you to take any positive action, it's not serving you.

Getting to know my thoughts has been useful. If I'm thinking something which is making me feel stressed or anxious or down, without motivating me towards taking some kind of action, I know it's not serving me and is worth re-framing.

But how exactly do you do this?

1. Question. The first thing to do is to question the negative thought. Ask yourself, is this really true?

2. Gather evidence. In order to find out, take your thoughts to court and seek out evidence to either support the thought or challenge it. If you can find even one tiny shred of evidence which disputes your thought, you can replace it with a more accurate one.

3. Replace inaccurate thoughts. To do that, ask yourself, what is a more factual way of looking at this?

Positive affirmations also help to reframe negative thoughts. For example, stating that 'I am good enough', and then seeking out evidence to support that new belief, has made a real difference to my stress levels and my confidence.

We see things from only one perspective based on a belief system which is simply based on thoughts we've repeated often, which aren't necessarily accurate. For example, thinking: 'I'm always late' could become: 'From now on I'll arrive on time to everything'. Or 'I can't do this, who am I kidding?' could be reappraised into: 'This is a challenge, but I am capable of anything I put my mind to'.

Be more present

Mindfulness is the practice of being more 'present', which decreases stress and anxiety, increases immune response and heart rate variability and activates the pre-frontal cortex (our thinking brain) and ability to self-regulate our emotions. Mindful meditation has been proven to reduce pain as well as stress and lead to fewer episodes of depression and greater self-awareness and alertness. The benefits are plenty and, in my view, anything that helps us get to know ourselves better, activates our calming and alertness mechanisms AND boosts our immune function is a must-do practice for eczema sufferers, especially when it comes to managing stress and flare-ups.

Interestingly, it's not only the relaxation response that mindfulness activates, but it also has the capacity to decrease rumination (when we dwell on our thoughts, regrets and so on). This is because it helps us to detach ourselves from what we are ruminating about, by focusing on the breath and our senses – what we can see, hear, and feel around us at any given moment. When we focus our attention on the moment, and only the moment, we can find a sense of inner calm. It centres us to connect to our senses instead of our thoughts.

Once we have centred ourselves we are ready to talk back to our mind chatter if needs be and, over time, as well as carving out new neural pathways, mindful meditation can even physically alter our cardiovascular system.

Another important stress-busting benefit is that when we take time to pause and reflect, we can find examples of similar stressful situations that we were able to get ourselves out of or manage. We've risen to many challenges, so by getting ourselves into a calm state we are better able to access that databank of memories to remind ourselves that we've got through worse situations, met tighter deadlines or recovered from previous flare-ups of eczema. I find this really useful when it comes to reminding myself that 'this too shall pass'. Stressful situations don't last forever, and nor will your eczema flare-ups.

Count your blessings

Gratitude is such a powerful positive emotion. According to Heart Math Institute Studies, using what positive psychologists call an 'appreciation intervention' significantly boosts the immune system, mood and vitality while decreasing stress and depression levels and blood pressure. An appreciation intervention is simply doing something which enables you to feel grateful and savour an experience.

Examples of such interventions include writing a thank you letter to someone, then delivering it and reading it out to them, playing 'gratitude table tennis' or 'catch' where you shout out something you're grateful for as you hit or catch the ball, or keeping a gratitude journal where you record your gratitude each day.

I remember everything in life I have to be grateful for, and actively write a list to ingrain it into my mind. Given that we have a negativity bias – focusing on the bad rather than the good – it's up to us to consciously choose to find and focus on the good, to counter that bias. Identifying what's good is a great way to take the wind out of stress's sails. For example, I'll often say, 'This situation is stressful, but it's made me realise what's important to me', or 'This is making me feel stressed, but now I know what I don't want to do with more clarity'. Using 'this is stressful but…' is a good way to find the silver lining.

I then list all the things I'm grateful for, and soon find myself in a much more positive frame of mind. Gratitude acts as a self-soother and self-encourager. Positive truths matter, so make sure you invest time in noticing and noting them.

Cultivate compassion

Everybody gets stressed and has their own triggers and stressors. The thing is, we don't always know what other people's are, nor do we know what they've had to deal with. As such, rather than respond to someone who has caused us offence in a defensive way, where we assume the worst and judge them as such, when we respond with compassion rather than assumption, it's easier to move on and let go off the angst they may have caused us to feel. We never know what battles other people are fighting.

Another way to reduce stress is to increase our self-compassion. As well as giving ourselves a break (to recharge), it's helpful to give ourselves a break by forgiving ourselves for whatever it is we're beating ourselves up about. Positive psychologists call this giving ourselves 'permission to be human'. This means accepting that we are far from perfect and that we will make plenty of mistakes on our journey. Giving ourselves such permission and showing ourselves compassion reduces the pressure of perfection and high expectations – a key cause of stress.

Know what matters most to you

What are your priorities? I remember seeing a video that featured a university lecturer pouring rocks into a jar. He asked if the jar was full. The students said it was but then he poured in some smaller rocks. He asked if it was full again and the students of course said that it was. Finally he poured in some sand and then some water. Now it really was full.

He told the class that life is like that jar, and that too many of us fill our jars with the sand and small rocks and water first, which leaves no room for the big rocks. But the big rocks represent what matters most, so we should strive to fill our lives with what matters first.

Stress often comes from the pressure to fit everything into our lives – from work responsibilities to family obligations and chores. We end up running around like a headless chicken without doing what really matters. Conversely, when we get to know what really matters to us, we can better prioritise and set up boundaries. This means we are able to spend more of our time doing what we want and able to say no when we need to, so our schedules don't become crammed with sand.

Note: one or more of these big rocks should be self-care, because we don't function well if we don't take time to take care of ourselves. Breaks enable us to reset and recharge so that we can accomplish what we aim to more effectively.

Get outdoors

Walk in nature, do some gardening, cycle somewhere, plant something. So many studies point to ecotherapy – ie getting out in nature –as a major mood-booster and way to combat stress, anxiety and depression. We'll explore this in more depth in the E of my HOPE Principles.

Get creative

Colouring has been credited as a wonderful way to manage stress and anxiety. It's a mindful exercise because you are focused on an activity on which you need to concentrate, so you're not thinking about anything else in that moment. There's a magical sense of achievement too that comes from making something.

Myself, I love scrapbooking – crafting a book full of appealing and meaningful images has a calming affect on me.

Be kind

Giving to others stimulates the reward centre of the brain, and therefore acts as a buffer to stress. That's a scientific fact. And when we work towards a purpose, as we'll learn in the P chapter of my HOPE Principles section, our feelings of self-worth and meaning increase.

Build a strong support network

Surrounding yourself with people you can rely on who can also rely on you is a key pillar of wellbeing. We're all in this together and when you know that other people have your back and are there for you, should the need arise, that can act as an automatic de-stressor.

Sharing your thoughts and frustrations about a situation can help defuse its power, and getting a second opinion and alternative perspective can also be useful when trying to solve a problem. As humans we are tribal beings, and that's why we are wired to seek out emotional support from other people. And, when we do that, it decreases the levels of cortisol.

It took me a long time to realise how much other people matter, but when I did, it significantly and positively impacted the management of my eczema.

"I can't promise to fix
all your problems,
but I can promise you
won't face them alone."

UNKNOWN

CHAPTER 5

Support

Happiness is something everyone strives for, but it's just a fleeting feeling – one of the many positive emotions we are equipped to feel. So, rather than focusing on that single feeling, it makes sense that, in order to truly flourish and live a good life, there is far more to consider and focus our efforts upon.

According to positive psychologists there are six core 'pillars' of wellbeing which provide a blueprint for a life well-lived. So, rather than merely focus on 'being happy', they suggest, in order to truly flourish and thrive in our lives, to truly maximise our level of wellbeing, we should be aware of these six pillars, which form the PERMA-V model of wellbeing, and strive to achieve them in our daily lives.

These measurable elements are:

1. Positive Emotion
2. Engagement
3. Relationships
4. Meaning
5. Accomplishment
6. Vitality

The Vitality element has only recently been included after positive psychology expert Emiliya Zhivotovskaya, founder of The Flourishing Center in New York, put forward that, without vitality (good nutrition, exercise, sleep hygiene), the other pillars aren't as effective. After all, you could be full of gratitude with supportive relationships, doing meaningful work and accomplishing goals, but if you are not looking after your body and mind and not getting enough sleep or eating healthily, the benefits would diminish.

We'll look more closely at how important sleep, exercise and eating habits are to wellbeing and to healing eczema in the following HOPE Principles chapters. We've also seen in Chapter Three how 'meaning' plays such an important part, as I discovered when I began pursuing my purpose in my career. Doing so has also ticked the 'engagement' and 'accomplishment' boxes for me, as I feel fully engaged by what I do, enjoy using my strengths to rise to the challenges that self-employment brings and feel accomplished with every goal met.

We'll also look more closely at some of the positive emotions, such as gratitude, and visualising our accomplishments in the HOPE Principles section of the book. For now, let's focus on 'Relationships'.

supportive relationships

Strong, supportive and rewarding social relationships are a critical pillar of wellbeing, and this has certainly been true for me. Over the past decade I've gradually realised just how much other people matter in my journey towards becoming eczema-free, and my overall sense of wellbeing too.

However, what I've found is that having people around you who care is one thing, but learning to open up to them and accept help from them is another.

When I look back over the past five years, the support I've gained from friends (once I'd opened up to them) and family (once I'd accepted help from them) has bolstered my healing power.

I say 'once I'd opened up' and 'accepted help', because opening up and accepting help was the turning point for me. But it took me two full years of receiving support from friends once I'd opened up to even fully realise the power of those supportive relationships.

the first seeds of support

Of course, I've been supported by my family my whole life, but we can so often take this unconditional support for granted. Although I have always appreciated the support my family have given me, I still chose an insular option where I'd spend time alone rather than be a burden to the ones I loved – and rather than reveal the true extent of my skin condition to friends.

Eczema can be very isolating, but isolation can be toxic for the mind. It was only once I started to let my friends in that I began to realise the power of other people. However, that realisation took a long while to sink in. Perhaps you can relate? We might notice and feel grateful for something in our lives, but we may not fully appreciate the impact immediately.

Realisation can take the journey of a border of growing plants. Initially a seed is sown and watered; more seeds are planted, and seedlings watered, until finally, some time later, the seedling grows into a flower. That flower represents the realisation – the 'a-ha moment' – and we continue to blossom and flourish from that moment onwards.

I've often found these 'a-ha moments' can take a while to fully integrate. I may notice something is making a difference, but then life will get in the way and I'll cast that notion aside. But life also has a habit of showing you time and time again what works and what doesn't, using your body as a signal to demonstrate. That's how the support lesson was learned – over time.

For example, I remember when I had just come out of hospital and felt incredibly lonely. Too scared to let my friends see what had happened to me, and too scared of speaking about my true suffering, I totally isolated myself. This was not healthy and not healing, and I highly recommend you don't do the same.

A few months after my hospital episode, I remember going to dinner with some dear friends. I wasn't myself because of all I'd been through, and everyone was asking me what I'd been up to and why I hadn't been texting them back. I decided to show two of the girls at the table what had happened to me that January, and their faces dropped with devastation. They said they couldn't believe they didn't know, and that I hadn't told them.

"We would have been there for you, Camille," they said, "if only we'd known."

They said they would have flown back to be with me. "We're your friends, Camille." And that's what friends do. I didn't realise how much people would have cared. It took me another couple of years to fully be comfortable with opening up to that vulnerable part of me, to show people the reality of my skin condition, bleeding raw skin and all, and to realise that when you do show people your true self and the battles you are fighting, people DO care. That was the first seed sown, which taught me the importance of supportive relationships.

When I found the courage to briefly let my friends in on what I was going through, they couldn't have been more supportive. With most of them living all over the world, they offered kind words of encouragement, told me not to give up and provided a safe space to open my heart up (through Skype). That was the first step to sharing the real me with people who cared about me.

If people see a perfect illusion of who you are, and only that illusion –what you/we all put out there on social media – they are less able to support you. Only when we show that vulnerability, that human-ness, do people show they truly care and understand, because that's when they get to see the whole picture, and that's when they relate to you and fully support you.

So, gradually, I began to open up. The next time my eczema began to flare up in 2015, I couldn't sleep at night, and the first thing I did was to call my friend Becky and open up. I cried down the phone to her, and she listened. She was 100% there for me. She worked for Emirates, so she got a flight somehow, and surprised me by turning up at my favourite café after her and my mum sneakily organised the surprise.

I will never forget that day. That kind act of friendship slowed down the eczema flare-up, but, most of all it poured water on that initial seed of knowledge: that I could reach out to people. Here was an option that I could take – a lifeline of people who would listen and be there, like a line of paper dolls, linking hands in loving support.

I had experienced support before this, though. Back in March 2013, although I was still suffering from eczema, it was starting to heal. And, as the spring began to sow its annual seeds of hope, the support I received gave me even more hope for the future. The seedlings of hope around this 'supportive relationships' pillar of wellbeing were slowly growing.

The next seed of hope came from Katie, who had begun working for Kris and had bought me crystals as a symbol of her friendship. I remember how much of an impact that one act of kindness had on me, and how having an ally who loved healthy food and who was on the same wavelength as me helped so much. I began to cook more and eat more and feel more comfortable in my own skin.

When my sister also showed her faith in me and in my healing, that also bolstered my belief in myself, and, as I said in Chapter Two, that support from my sister provided the catalyst for me gradually accepting support from others too.

However, while I became more open to accepting support from my friends and family, the penny still hadn't dropped that this support was as vital a part of the healing jigsaw as food and exercise were.

Indeed, it wasn't until two years later, in March 2015, when I went to London to heal that the seedlings began to grow into flowers of realisation. It was that time when the massage therapist refused to massage me, because my skin had flared up so much, when my friends were saying, 'You're in London, why aren't you calling us?'.

I told them what was going on, and let them know I was there, but I also said I didn't want to see anyone. I reverted to my insular approach as I still felt ashamed and scared of how they might react, and just wanted to stay in my cocoon and not be a burden on anyone. I was acting like a seedling that hid from the nourishing water and sunshine and buried itself back down into the soil. That's not the right conditions for growth or flourishing – that's going backwards.

And of course, that's not how true friendship rolls, is it? We want to be there for our friends, and be there for me they were.

accepting support

Yes, I'm so fortunate to be able to say my true friends have always been there for me. If only I had noticed that sooner and been brave enough to share the whole truth with them. Because, once I did, I blossomed.

Once I'd let people know about my situation and where I was, one friend, Joey, turned up at my hotel door and said, 'Let's have a cup of peppermint tea'. I replied, in surprise, 'But, look at me!" And he said we could just chat. I'll always appreciate his support. As a result of his encouragement, I learned from him that "life comes to those who put themselves out there".

The next day a girlfriend, Lamara, rang me. 'Right, we're having dinner,' she said, and I agreed. I let her in and those two branches of support acted as a catalyst for me to let others in too. From that moment onwards I felt the support of people, just coming and spending time with me, healed me more than not seeing anyone and just drinking juice.

Just juicing hadn't worked at all for me the first time and yet I had been stubborn in my devotion to the juicing programme. I remember, back then, my boyfriend at the time had invited me out to dinner, but I said I couldn't, because I was juicing. I was in that much pain and was so desperate for it to end, I thought maybe juicing was the answer, so I'd go at it, full force and would deny myself the company of people I loved – denying myself one of the core pillars of wellbeing.

Everything for me was about not eating, because I had to juice, as if 'nothing else existed' other than juice work. Not only was that a limiting and restrictive way to live my life, it also failed to work. I still flared up often during those juice-only periods and, when I did, my eczema lasted and took a long time to heal.

But guess what? I haven't flared up anywhere near as frequently or for as long ever since I accepted and cultivated and nourished the support in my life: evidence that supportive relationships really do work.

the power of love

From the consistent unconditional love and support offered by my mother who is always there and never gives up on me, to the

128

consistent love and belief in me offered by my father, who has always wanted me to learn as much as possible through him and for me not to suffer.

From the support of my grandma who knitted my mittens and taught me to never give up when life gets tough, and my grandad who told me my eczema didn't make me ugly and that it wouldn't last forever – he was right.

From the deep encouragement from my brother Dominic, who has never let me give up on my dreams, thank you for listening to me and making me giggle when I over-think life. And the incredible loyalty from my sister Rochelle who is my true other half and makes me feel strong, like I can take on the world with her by my side.

From my youngest brother Benjamin, who recently inspired me with his phrase, "When you don't want to do something, it's probably the thing you really need to do". You are wise beyond your years.

From my understanding boyfriend Baz, my partner through life who gets me lemon tea, takes me on walks in the fresh air and reminds me I am stronger than my skin condition, to my best friends in the UK, America, Canada, Palma, Malta and New Zealand who have cheered me on every step of the way and all the moments in between, they have showed up and supported me.

I consider myself to be very lucky to be the daughter of such beautiful souls, the sister of such wonderful siblings and to be the friend of so many amazing human beings. There are too many to mention here, but I've shared so much with my friends – we've shared our anxieties, our health magazines, our love for pampering and our laughter, we've been on road trips and daily adventures; from running buddies and yoga-moon-loving-besties to strong girls who've held my hands when I've reached to scratch myself, or leant me their ears and given me contagious positive energy when I've struggled to cope.

From the caring boys who've sent me inspirational quotes and positive playlists, and the wonderful women who've sent me self-care boxes filled with colouring books and natural skincare products, just when I've needed them most. I feel privileged to have each and every one of these people in my life. Even Roxy, my sister's cat, has always given me cuddles and unconditional love. And all of that love and support is part of the healing recipe. Yes, support is a crucial ingredient.

For me, it had been there all along, but until I recognised its power, I hadn't put it into the healing mixture. Now, whenever I get a flare-up, I refer to my checklist and make sure I carve out some time to spend with my support network, as well as eating well and sleeping well. I look at which ingredients are missing or which I need to add more of, and I bake myself a self-care pie with all of those yummy ingredients. Supportive relationships are the cherry on the self-care cake.

being with friends

Talking of food... Before my trip to London I noticed that, despite eating more healthily, my eczema was still persisting, so I had visited a naturopathic doctor. I told him how I couldn't understand why I was still getting flare-ups despite my incredibly healthy diet.

And he said, 'Camille, your diet couldn't be any more perfect. But a perfect meal eaten alone is more toxic than a not so healthy meal eaten with friends.' Boom! That was a big awakening and opened the doors towards my acceptance of support when it showed up during my trip to London. I'm so glad my friends persisted in showing up for me.

I had grown accustomed to eating alone back at university, because I didn't want anyone to see what I ate after people had previously made snide remarks about what I was eating. But now, when I'm with friends and I'm not eating as healthily as I might have liked, or there's a bit of butter in something – which is dairy – I don't freak out. I just look at the company I've got and how nourishing that is to my soul. That makes me feel so grateful for my meal that I'll eat it and feel so content with that nourishment, as opposed to alone, sipping a juice.

re-writing the stories we tell ourselves

I could have saved myself so much pain had I realised the positive impact of opening up to friends and family earlier. This notion of advocating for yourself, of sharing what you need from others with them and asking for support when you need it, that's so critical to living a good life, and a healthy one.

However, it's been a useful exercise to reflect back on that two-year period when the seeds of knowledge were first planted and then flowered into full bloom and realisation. Although I wish I'd realised the power of supportive relationships sooner, I also feel that the mistakes we make and the most uncomfortable times we experience provide the biggest opportunities for learning.

So when I reflect back on the journey of the seeds of knowledge, that's when I truly learned that supportive relationships matter more than I'd given them credit for. Then, to later discover that positive psychologists and researchers have found this to be true was a wonderful way to cement the evidence that I'd discovered myself. I'd been telling myself the story that my friends wouldn't want the burden of knowing the truth and were probably too busy to help and that I was better off coping on my own by juicing and eating well and keeping myself to myself – but over two years I began to gather evidence to the contrary.

The seeds of support being a healthy part of the jigsaw were first sown back in March 2013 after hospital, when I finally admitted to my friends that I'd been hospitalised with my eczema. Until then they had no idea how bad it had got.

More seeds of support as a healing strategy were sown that spring when Katie and I were working together.

That seedling was watered in London, two years after the first seed was sown, when I started opening up and letting my friends help me.

But, it wasn't until the following spring (2015) that I knew 100 per cent that support was an integral part of the healing journey – a prime puzzle piece.

So now, I've been able to write a new story which serves me a whole lot better. Over time, this realisation of the power of support replaced the fear of 'what will they think?' and the feeling of having to cope alone. Now, if eczema flares up, and I feel like I'm losing track of everything I've learned, I make the effort to talk to someone, to my sister, my friends or my mum, and now to my dad too.

In the past I'd seen my eczema as a weakness and would never have opened up to my dad about all that was going on with it. But now I'll share how I'm feeling with him and also get his perspective if I do get a flare-up, to see if he can see what he think might be causing it. Those who know us best are the best sounding boards and providers of guidance whenever we feel like we are straying off course or when something is troubling us.

When we share our reality and our whys – our reasons for taking certain approaches to healing and living, and even reveal ourselves when we're at our worst (for example, showing our skin to people when it's at its most painful), we get to find out who is there for us and who isn't, and we have more chance of fostering some level of understanding from those who are less reluctant to offer support.

On the whole though, I recommend only spending time with the people who lift you up and fully support you. There's no point trying to spend time persuading people why you are doing what you are doing unless they get it. Some people will just think you don't need to change what you are doing, because they don't get it. And you don't owe an explanation to those people. But you do to your friends and the family who support you, because they WANT to be there for you. That's part of the remit of true friendship and love.

know yourself and know who knows you best

The words my brother Dominic shared with me are a case in point. On his 19th birthday my brother reminded me of the strong fighter I was. I had Skyped him to wish him a happy birthday and put on a brave face, but, being my brother and knowing me so well, he could see straight through me. He reminded me of the girl who used to jump out of bed early mornings to go out running; the girl who was a jet-setter but never got jet-lag. He asked me what had happened to that girl?

He knows me so well that he knew how to motivate me to run again when I'd stopped doing so because of the pain of my eczema.

"Camille," he said, "you were put on this earth to be challenged. The only thing that you can control is your mind – take control of that and all will be right again. Now get yourself on a run like the Camille I know." It was at moment that I remembered I hadn't run in months due to a knee injury. The knee injury I sustained while running a half marathon had healed while I was in Israel, and his supportive words gave me the motivation to regain control over that part of my life. I jumped out of bed, pulled my trainers on and went running. Being active has been a crucial part of my healing journey ever since.

Learning what is best for you can take a lot of time, and what's best for one person isn't necessarily what's best for other people. So self-care is about self-awareness first. The more you know yourself, accept yourself and support yourself, the more you'll know what you need from others, what will nourish you most. This means you are better able to know the kind of friendships you want, how much love and support you're going to give yourself, and what you expect from other people.

Different people provide different types of support. When you know yourself, you know what support you need most and when. For example, my boyfriend is amazing. He's great at instantly knowing what to do. If I start feeling like my skin is having a flare-up, he'll say 'Right, we're going for a walk', or 'I'm taking us for dinner', or 'let's look into moving abroad near the sea'.

My family are amazing at distracting me by inviting me to do something fun to take my mind off things and pulling my focus away from it, because there's more to life than worrying about a flare-up. My best friends are amazing at listening and helping me talk through problems and solutions and ideas. Each of these people show up in a different way, and this helps me choose who to call depending on what I need most at any given time.

I don't believe your support system has to be a group of people suffering with eczema too. Just people who understand your condition does affect you, who are therefore able to be sensitive about it; but more so are a joy to be around, so they can take your mind off your eczema.

Don't expect the world from other people – if you reach out, and people aren't supportive, that's okay. Just know that there will be people who will listen to you and encourage you and will be your rock in life. That's what I've found to be true.

And, for people who feel isolated, or who don't feel like they have that support network yet, I felt like that once. Although I spent so much time seeking it, I couldn't find any positive online advice in the online eczema communities. They were filled with people suffering, and I wanted to read about people who had overcome their eczema and how they had done so. Being unable to find any support online led me to write this book – to share a more positive story about how I've gained control over my eczema, as opposed to my eczema controlling me.

I now feel there is more support online through Instagram. By talking about my condition I have attracted friends of friends to reach out and talk to me, and have even developed new friendships via social media through our mutual suffering of eczema. So, if you are struggling to build your support network, start with the people who follow my page – there is support out there if you know where to look.

I also recommend going to empowering events alone. I recently went to a Hay House Ignite event alone. Jessie, a clairvoyant I met through Instagram, introduced me to some incredible like-minded women. I was able to share my spirituality with these women, which helped unlock a part of myself that I had hidden away for so long. It also reignited my trust in the universe again.

I went to another event, the Mel Wells' Self Love Summit, with my new friend Vanessa and best friend Gemma. I had never been surrounded by so many kind, loving and empowering women in one room before. It helped me 'let go' of not fitting into a girl group in high school. It showed me there is an authentic, supportive girl tribe out there for me, and there is for you too! I hope this book will also provide you with the support you need.

the science of social support

Physical presence and touch has been proven to positively affect us. It has a calming effect on us when people provide us with comfort and connection. When someone offers us a hug or a shoulder to cry on, a reassuring hand on ours or a friendly rub on the back, we release oxytocin into our brains and bodies and decrease the amount of cortisol, the stress hormone. Evidently social support in the physical sense has a very positive effect on our wellbeing and our sense that 'everything is going to be all right'.

But emotional support is just as important as physical support and informational support (where we are given advice, and able to discuss solutions with others). Emotional support, ie empathy, care and trust that we gain from others, is hugely valuable. This is because, as humans, we have an intrinsic need to belong. We are social animals and other people have the power to lift us up or bring us down. So, it's important to choose your support network wisely with this in mind.

According to studies of over 100,000 participants across 49 countries, researchers Helliwell and Putnam discovered that trusted reciprocal social connections significantly positively impacted happiness and life satisfaction. Meanwhile, Friedman and Martin reported more recently that "having friendships has the highest positive correlation with happiness". So, supportive relationships with other people has more of an impact on our overall wellbeing than any other factor.

The converse is also true, because loneliness is worse for us than stress. Some research even points to loneliness weakening the immune system, with chronic isolation being as big a risk factor in mortality as smoking.

There have even been tests on patients with leukaemia who were preparing to undergo bone marrow transplants. A 2011 study by the Mount Sinai School of Medicine found that 54% of those with strong emotional support were alive two years later, compared to just 20% of those with little social support from friends and family.

Another experiment in 1997 saw 276 participants quarantined for five days and given flu nasal spray. Gender, race, age and smoking habits were all taken into consideration, and those with the most supportive social connections were less likely to catch a cold, and produced less mucus if they did. Meanwhile, multiple studies show that supportive relationships have the power to significantly calm the cardiovascular system, lowering stress hormones and blood pressure.

All of this makes sense to me when I think about how isolated I felt during the worst points in my eczema journey. I had shut myself off from support, so it was self-induced isolation; eating alone, keeping myself to myself, hiding myself away and coping on my own. Equally, when I reflect on what have been the happiest moments of my life, relationships played an important role in those moments. They feature other people, friends and family.

Work studies have also shown that even brief moments of positive interactions with other people can improve working memory and cognitive performance. We can think and perform better when we feel supported. What's more, according to Heaphy and

Dutton, such positive interactions can boost our immune system. From a health perspective as an eczema sufferer, anything that boosts the immune system is a good thing.

Whatever way you look at it, the healing power of supportive relationships is immense. When you're on a journey of self-healing, it's so important to own who you are and open up to the people you love about living with eczema.

So how will you cultivate the relationships and nourish the friendships that lift you up?

How will you develop new friendships with like-minded people?

And what will you do about those who pull you down?

I now do activities where I can meet more like-minded people, and thus my circle and confidence increase. I only surround myself with people who lift me up. We all live busy lives, but I do what I can to schedule Skype calls and, although life can get in the way, now that I know how important relationships are to my wellbeing and health (and to that of my friends of family), I am more ready to prioritise friendships whenever possible. Obviously life is a balancing act of being busy with work and so on, but friends understand when you are busy, and a simple text wishing love can be enough until you next connect more fully.

Ultimately, only when we surround ourselves with the right support network and nurture those connections with compassion and kindness can we fully heal.

befriending ourselves

Equally important is being kind to our own minds; treating ourselves like we treat our best friends. Supporting ourselves with self-compassion is a critical piece of the wellbeing jigsaw puzzle. When we befriend ourselves, see ourselves as our childhood selves and turn down the volume of our internal critical radio station, we can pause our self-judgement and self-criticism and replace it with self-awareness and self-compassion.

It's important to give ourselves permission to mess up sometimes and to give ourselves the kind of break that we'd encourage our friends to give themselves if they're beating themselves up.

But it's tough to come from that self-compassionate place.

When my eczema flares up, it can leave me feeling paralysed and make me question whether I am capable of helping people. Luckily, I've learned as a result of developing my self-awareness and self compassion that this is simply me having a bad day, and that I need to ramp up my self-care.

Of course, I know I am capable as I quickly bounce back from these flare-ups with my self-care tools. Yet even now I'm living my dream career life, I still get worn out and stressed, because I'm human. So it's important to give myself permission to be so.

It has been hard creating this book, my website and YouTube videos, as I have had to re-live the pain I went through and put myself out there – not only opening up to my friends and family, but to strangers too. I also have days where I don't feel strong enough to share my story, and it makes me physically break down.

The fear of being judged and mocked used to play on my mind at night. And I still have days where I worry if I am being a good enough family member, friend, girlfriend. I can be critical of my body too.

However, these are during my BAD days, and thankfully they don't last long at all any more. But this is only because I have my checklist and have developed, as a result, my HOPE Principles – which provide me with guidance and help me to tap into my self-awareness, self-compassion and self-care when I most need it.

Over the following pages, I'll share my HOPE Principles with you.

CHAPTER 6

H is for Home

Where you are at any given time is important. I mean that in a number of ways. Where you are physically – at home, at work, at the gym/pub/park, on a beach, in a field, wherever you are – the location, the environment and who you're surrounded by – all of this can have an impact on your wellbeing. But so too can where you are emotionally, ie where you are in terms of where your head is at.

For example, are you spending a lot of time ruminating on the past, worrying about the future or focused on the present? While it's good to reminisce on happy memories and visualise a happy future, it's not helpful to regret the past or get anxious about the future; the best place to focus on is right now. And that's why mindfulness – the art of 'noticing now', has become so popular as a life-coping and wellbeing boosting strategy.

This chapter will explore how we can use where we are to our advantage to boost wellbeing and manage eczema, or any other challenges we may face – both in terms of our internal and external environment. We'll address our actual location and our mental location.

Yes, our environment can significantly impact our happiness and, as I've discovered, can be beneficial or detrimental to skin conditions. And so can where we are in our heads.

When I look back over my own experiences, I realise that a number of environmental and cultural factors have affected me. The drinking culture at university was counter-productive to my healthy lifestyle and, having experienced six months in sunny California, it became clear that the English winters didn't feel particularly good either.

While I do try to escape to sunnier climates whenever I can, it's not always possible to do so. So, rather than complain about these environmental factors, I've chosen to acknowledge when I'm not in the best environment for myself and then do what I can to make the most of where I am, at any given time. During colder months, I ramp up the self-care and I make sure that I'm optimising whatever environment I'm in by focusing on my inner environment, so that I can feel good whatever the weather or circumstances.

Therefore, this chapter is about creating the right environment at home and creating the right environment in our heads. Improving our home environment isn't simply about replacing bedsheets and pillows with anti-allergy materials (although that is still important). It's about a combination of:

- de-cluttering, both in the literal sense in our homes and in a psychological sense in our minds;
- getting sufficient sleep that we have enough energy to cope with life;
- coming home to ourselves, by creating sanctuaries for mindfulness meditation and calm reflection, both within the home and outside it.

So let's look at each of these areas one by one, as these factors can have a big impact on both our internal and external environment.

de-cluttering

Our outer world can strongly affect our inner world. When we're surrounded by external clutter and mess, it can transport into our heads and create a mess there too. It makes sense to de-clutter, because, by de-cluttering our homes we can de-clutter our minds. It literally restores our mental energy.

Just as we can give ourselves a boost by replacing activities that don't matter to us with activities that do, such as swapping scrolling through social media with reading more books, (more on that in the Purpose chapter later) we can also clear out the stuff we own that doesn't matter to make room for what does matter in our homes. When you de-clutter, you literally give yourself breathing space and more mental energy to deal with whatever comes your way.

"Have nothing in your house that you do not know to be useful or believe to be beautiful."
William Morris

Creating a de-cluttering routine is helpful. For me, every Sunday I play positive music while I clear my room from the weekly clutter which piles up. I burn sage or incense to clear the air, and open all the windows to let some fresh air in.

144

Whenever I want to have an even deeper de-clutter, I use this plan of action to get me from oppressive mess to de-stressed. Notice that the de-cluttering session doesn't end when everything has been put away (or put in a pile for donation/dump or sale). There's an extra and equally important step at the end.

Step 1: Give everything a home

Visit a charity shop or your favourite homewares store to get some storage boxes and paper files if you need to. Then plan where you intend to put and keep certain items, as it saves time and is easier to stay on top of everything when everything has its place.

Have a clutter box to dump anything that doesn't have a place currently. You can deal with that at the end of your de-cluttering session.

Step 2: Tackle dump zones

These are those places where you might dump paperwork, stuff to take upstairs, such as tables, sideboards, the stairs and so on. Clear these first by putting paperwork in folders, getting rid of anything that doesn't 'spark joy' in you and putting everything else away in its proper place. There is a book called *Spark Joy* which I have been told is an amazing book to read on de-cluttering.

Step 3: Tackle your home room by room

I tend to start with the kitchen, then the lounge, then bedrooms and bathroom. Your aim is to get rid of as much as possible, so have a box or bin liner for the charity shop or dump and a 'to sell' pile.

Drawer-by-drawer, shelf-by-shelf, go through everything and be as ruthless as possible. Anything you haven't used for six to nine months, you don't need. I try to de-clutter my wardrobe every season and give my clothes to friends or charity.

Step 4: Empty your clutter box and create a space for anything within it

Give a home to batteries, a place for elastic bands. Once everything is in its place, your de-cluttering is almost complete.

Step 5: Create a serene space

Now you've created more breathing space, why not create a space in which to breathe – a comfortable chair with a beautiful cushion or pillow, a nice lamp or vase with flowers in? Perhaps an aromatherapy candle? Your favourite books or magazines, a luxury notebook and pen and a picture frame with a photograph of your favourite people in it? House plants to improve air quality? Anything that makes you feel good.

This is your reward for de-cluttering. Perhaps you could spend any money you've made from selling stuff that was cluttering up your home on making this serenity space extra special.

sleeping well

Energy and wellbeing are intrinsically linked. The more energy we have, the more able we are to focus on whatever we need to do. Our self-control is heightened and we simply feel better.

The more tired we feel, the less able we are to concentrate and get stuff done. Life is altogether harder when we're tired. When children are tired they cry and get grumpy and, frankly, no matter what age you are, it's harder to cope with life when we're low on energy.

How we treat ourselves has a lot to answer for when it comes to energy levels. The food we put into our bodies matters, the amount we move our bodies matters, and also how much rest and recuperation we give our bodies matters.

Sleep is an important restorative process in which our bodies rest and repair muscles and support immune functions. Meanwhile, our brains process our memories, and our dreams help us to work through our worries. As such, sleep helps to restore our mind and body effectively. Some studies have even revealed that we are more likely to remember negative memories rather than positive ones when we don't get enough sleep, and we are more sensitive to negative experiences when we're sleep deprived. We also experience worse cravings for unhealthy food when we're tired, and our self-control can be affected too.

Fundamentally, sleep affects our mood, feelings, performance, willpower, hunger, emotional response and immune response.

I know when I fall into stress it is usually from lack of sleep. When this happens, I prioritise rest above anything else. I make sure to go to bed earlier and spray lavender oil to help induce sleep.

Sometimes, of course, I find myself going to bed late, which is not an ideal situation. But, the way I see it, if I can try to aim for the 80/20 rule and get to bed at a decent time 80 per cent of the time, I'm more likely to get the recommended seven to eight hours. Striving for perfection can be detrimental to our mental health, so I give myself permission to be human and do what I can.

I know that getting extra sleep is beneficial to me, as it is for everyone. It's especially important for eczema sufferers, as sleep loss fuels inflammation and inflammation fuels eczema, so it's a vicious cycle. I remember back in 2012 when I moved back to England from California, it was a harsh cold winter. I had started a new job with a 2-hour commute, and I was losing so much sleep 'worrying' my alarm wouldn't go off. I look back now and think what mental torture I used to put myself through. The lack of sleep was a huge contribution to my eczema exploding out of control.

Over the years I've learnt how vital sleep is for my overall wellbeing, and have worked on how to make sure I can get the best night's rest.

Create a sleep schedule

Try to go to bed at the same time each night and wake at the same time each day. Having a sleep schedule really helped me. It gets your body into a routine of what time to wake up and what time to wind down for sleep. I try to go to bed around 11pm and wake up at 7am to get a good eight hours.

Create a bedtime ritual

This is mine:

- An hour or two before I want to fall asleep, I try not to use my phone or watch TV, and choose a good book to read. My favourite is *You Can Heal Your Life* by Louise Hay. I find myself far more sleepy when I choose to read before bed, rather than scroll through social media. If you find this impossible, try installing an app on your phone which reduces the blue light, such as Twilight. Research has found that melatonin, the hormone which promotes sleep, is suppressed by blue light, so the less you look at screens before bed, the better.
- I enjoy a bath full of Epsom salts and castor oil, and then pamper myself with a natural moisturiser whilst listening to a meditation or inspirational speaker, or reciting my affirmations in my head and visualising my future.
- I do a mini yoga flow to get me into a state of peace. I then write a few sentences in my gratitude journal to reflect on what went well in the day, and what I hope will go well in the week to come.
- I drink a glass of Natural Calm Magnesium, and drift off. This always works a treat for me. Stress can be a cause of magnesium deficiency, and vice versa, stress depletes your magnesium levels. Magnesium is abundant in lots of leafy vegetables, and is also very high in cacao powder, probably why I love eating raw chocolate so much! I am naturally a very driven, ambitious person that likes to

149

push my own limits. However, this mental willpower could quickly tip me over the 'stress edge', so I like to keep my magnesium levels in check with the Natural Calm supplement. You can get it in many different flavours and I love having it as part of my bedtime ritual. It genuinely makes me feel calm, and I wouldn't go a night without it. They even do 'travel packets' which are useful for when I am on the go.

Be prepared

Make sure the room is dark, uncluttered and cool. Have a cold flannel next to your bed, just in case you ever wake with the burning desire to scratch your skin. Breathe deeply to help you relax. I used to do this all the time and it really helped. Afterwards I would spray colloidal silver on my skin to soothe the irritation and provide healing to whatever is burning up under my skin.

coming home to yourself ~ creating sanctuaries of meditation and reflection

We've spoken quite a bit about inner and outer health– from the outer barrier of our skin to the inner functionality of our immune system, and from the outer environment affecting our inner environment. During my own journey I've discovered that my external actions deeply affect my inner peace– that sense of calm reassurance that is available to us all.

The problem is, we often live such busy lives, tuning in to that inner peace isn't always easy. But, when we do, it can be like flicking on a control switch over our lives.

Some say that mindfulness is about 'waking up to life'. For me, it's about noticing what I can hear, see, feel, touch or taste in any given moment; becoming more present within the present. It doesn't come easily, as our autopilot response is to ruminate on the past or ponder on the future, but, with practice, it gets easier.

Noticing our environment – what's around us at any given moment – is a key part of mindfulness. Really paying attention to everything– from the sound of the birds tweeting to the gentle whisper of the breeze in the trees –can really nourish us and bring us out of our autopilot setting into one that better serves our wellbeing and flicks our inner peace switch on.

Various studies have shown that being mindful can significantly reduce stress, depression and anxiety and improve concentration levels, pain management and sleep. But what does it entail?

Well, mindfulness isn't about relaxing or switching off, it's about being present. Savouring each moment and action– slowing down to appreciate the taste and sensation of what you are eating, paying attention to each of your senses and what you are feeling and experiencing and sensing in any given moment.

Meanwhile, meditation is part of the mindfulness toolkit which can help you to get grounded enough to boost your awareness and capacity for mindfulness. Meditation is not mindfulness; it's about focusing on your breath to better connect with yourself.

Since I've been practising both meditation (focusing on the breath or affirmations) and mindfulness (noticing now), I've found that I'm better able to cope with what life throws at me. As well as enabling me to tap into my inner peace, it has helped me to appreciate my outer world and gain a deeper understanding about how best to cope with the outer stimuli that I respond to throughout each day. For example, if I find myself getting in a pickle about my eczema, focusing on what else surrounds me is a great distraction, while meditation enables me to come home to myself and access my appreciation for all that is good in my life, despite any eczema.

During my meditation sessions I often use affirmations to centre my thoughts. This means, if I find my mind wandering to thoughts about what I ought to be doing or something I've said to someone, I bring my mind back first to my breath: "in… two, three, four…. Hold, two, three, four… Out… two, three, four" –and then to my affirmation.

I tend to use affirmations to help focus my mind on the outcome I want, instead of the condition I might be in. I used them a lot more when I was covered in eczema. I would look in the mirror, deep into my eyes, and say, 'I AM WELL', 'I AM HEALED' and 'I LOVE YOU'.

This isn't as easy as it sounds when you have been dodging the mirror, afraid of what you may see. When you face yourself in the mirror for the first time in a while, you see your truth. I remember looking at heartbroken, scared and hurting eyes – but somehow the more I looked and said these powerful words, the more I believed them. There is something extremely healing when you look into your own eyes and say the kind words you so lovingly deserve. We've been looking in the mirror at ourselves and at our own eyes ever since we were children, and we can connect to ourselves in a really deep and loving way.

In *You Can Heal Your Life* by Louise Hay, founder of Hay House Publishing, she lists many affirmations for different ailments. Reading that book helped me to feel less alone. I still frequently play Louise Hay meditations whilst I soak in a salt bath. I find listening to them helps me calm my mind, no matter how my day has gone.

As well as listening to guided meditations in the bath or before bed (Insight Timer is a great guided meditation app to try out), I also try to create a sanctuary of meditation and reflection wherever I am. At home I have an area where I sit, but if I go away on holiday I hone in on a corner or area that I can go to sit and be still – to find that sense of inner peace and get present.

Being mindful isn't only about being aware of the good feelings. It can also mean noticing and 'leaning in' to the negative feelings and thoughts that come up, without any sense of judgement, just acceptance. That in itself is empowering.

We can't change the past, nor can we know what the future holds, but we can control how we respond in each moment – in a mindful or a mindless way. That's a choice we make in every moment of every day. Since I've been choosing the former, I've found it easier to control my response to what happens to me.

Sanctuaries of meditation and reflection need not only be within your home. They can be anywhere. Here are a few ways I try to bring mindfulness into my environment, wherever I may be.

Mindful grounding

If I can take my shoes and socks off, I do so and firmly place my feet on the ground. I spend a few minutes noticing the sensation of my bare feet on the ground, tuning in to my sense of touch. I notice how sturdy the ground is or how soft the grass or sand is. This process makes me feel grounded, stable and secure as I feel it flowing up my body from my feet.

Mindful breathing

Wherever you are, you can stop what you are doing and focus on your breathing. I often use box breathing – breathing in for the count of four, holding for four – but I sometimes play around with breathing out for longer counts than I breathe in for, if I want to feel calm.

Mindful music

I like to listen to music and tune in to every single note, to each instrument and melody. This mindful listening is a wonderful way to focus on now. I then focus on how my body is feeling in that moment, which expands my awareness.

Mindful mouthfuls

When I'm eating I try to savour every single mouthful, but, more than that, I notice the flavour on my tastebuds as I slowly chew. I tune in to the taste. I've found this has helped me to really appreciate what I'm eating more. We so often chow down whatever is in front of us, especially when we're hungry, hardly noticing the taste or sensation of it as we swallow. But noticing what happens when we chew can help to turn each meal into a delight.

Wherever we are in the world, we can bring ourselves back to our breath, and to our selves, and to the moment. This helps us to cherish and savour more moments, but also helps us to gain more control over our minds and reactions to life. As Cheryl Rickman says in *The Flourish Handbook*, mindfulness and meditation can also act as a kind of "emotional energy pit stop".

I'm all for anything that boosts our energy and enables calm, because that provides a great foundation for boosting our positivity.

"Life is 10% what happens to you and 90% how you react to it."

CHARLES SWINDOLL

CHAPTER 7

O is for Optimism

response is everything

Reaction is better than cure. I've found this to be so true. How I react to what is happening to my body has the power to either lift me up or pull me down. And how I react is a choice. I didn't choose to have eczema, but I can control how I react to it.

I've found that the more I worry about my skin condition, the worse it gets. This makes my worries completely counter-productive. And there's some science to back this up.

According to Barbara Fredrickson, who has been studying the science of positivity for the past couple of decades, and neuro-scientist Rick Hanson, negative emotions (fear, anger, anxiety) close our minds, while positive emotions (gratitude, love, joy) open them.

Barbara has developed the 'broaden and build' theory, which explains how positivity improves our cognitive ability – so we think more clearly and make better decisions – in contrast to negativity, which diminishes our cognitive ability so our thinking becomes narrow and focused only on the problems and protecting ourselves from danger.

Worrying adversely affects our cognitive ability because, when we are in that mode of thinking, our rational mind is not in control. Our emotional mind is. This makes us closed off and less able to come up with solutions to the problems we're actually worrying about.

I've definitely experienced this myself. When I've spent a long time worrying about my eczema, I've struggled to find ways to heal, and the worry-induced stress I've created has actually made my eczema worse.

That's why reaction is so important and an integral part of the healing process. It's not easy, but we can learn how to respond well.

"In life, we cannot always control the first arrow. However, the second arrow is our reaction to the first. The second arrow is optional."
Buddha

We can choose how to react; whether to fire a second arrow. Sometimes we need to blow off some steam, to let our negative emotions flow and then go.

I think it's important not to bottle up or suppress negative emotions, but to accept them and even voice them. According to psychologists, when we label our negative feelings we gain control over them, and also defuse them. There have been various studies which show that when we name how we are feeling, we give those feelings less weight and end up feeling better more quickly. So simply by saying, 'I'm feeling angry and frustrated', those feelings start to dissipate, and we can move on.

The problem is when we let negative emotions fester; when we dwell on our circumstances. Especially the ones we can't do anything about. I've found that when something is bothering me now, I think about whether it's something within or outside of my control. If it's within my control, I list what I can do about it to stop it from bothering me. If it's outside of my control, I say how I'm feeling about it and why it's bothering me, and then I try to let it go. It doesn't always work. I'm only human but, most of the time, this works.

The problem is, our brains sometimes don't let our rational thinking side in.

When I began to approach the things I got stressed about from this perspective of 'is it within or outside of my control', I realised that how I respond to stressful situations (whether it's itchy eczema, an annoying colleague, or bad news) is within my control, even if the situation itself might not be.

So, in order to take charge of how to react, I seized control by reading up on how the brain works. And here is what I found out.

our protective brain

In order to protect us, our emotional brain (the amygdala) assumes control whenever it senses danger, even if that danger is imagined rather than real. When that natural fight or flight tendency takes hold, it's really difficult for any sense or logic to make it through to our thinking brain (the pre-frontal cortex). So, whenever our brain feels the need to protect us, we end up freaking out, getting all worked up, and imagining the worse-case scenario as our emotional brain spirals out of control.

Ironically, we end up as slaves to our irrational emotional side just when we need our rational thinking side the most. And when we're in that emotional fight or flight response mode, as the 'broaden and build theory' and other studies have shown, we are less able to think clearly, so less likely to come up with solutions to the problems or imagined dangers we're worrying about in the first place.

But why does our brain, with its good intentions of wanting to protect us, end up hampering our ability to cope?

Turns out it's to do with evolution and biology. Back when dangers lurked around every corner, we needed to be extra cautious. Far better to freak out and run away from something that wasn't there than to ignore something scary that was! But, now that dangers are lesser, our brains don't realise that and remain on high alert. So we still respond with our emotional brain and get ourselves into pickles about all kinds of stuff that we needn't be stressing about.

We also tend to focus on the negative rather than the positive as a result of the way our brains are wired.

So, the best way to counter all of this is to:

1. focus on what's good rather on what's bad, whenever we can and as often as we can;
2. breathe and get mindful, as this calms our emotional brain and lets our thinking brain resume control;
3. get moving, as this also helps to reset our brain and releases all kinds of feel-good chemicals too.

By ramping up the self-care, exercising and tapping into the power of ecotherapy, we can equip ourselves to cope with anything within and outside of our control in a more measured and effective way.

The HOPE Principles cover all of these. This chapter focuses on the O part of the HOPE Principles: on opting for optimism and gratitude and positivity to counter the inner freaker-outer that we all have to varying degrees.

optimistic or pessimistic?

When I started looking into how the brain works, I discovered something called 'explanatory style'. Most of us tend to have either an optimistic explanatory style or a pessimistic explanatory style. Our own explanatory style basically defines how we explain what is happening to us – ie who we tend to blame for what goes right or wrong, and whether we see the stuff we get right or wrong as temporary or long-lasting; specific to that one occasion or more pervasive.

If you see the glass half empty, you tend to see problems as your fault and achievements as down to other people or a fluke. You see those problems as likely to last for a long time, and think 'this kind of thing always happens to me', while successes are seen as temporary and as 'never usually happening to me' because the good stuff happens to other people.

When good stuff does happen, those with a pessimistic explanatory style tend to see these experiences as isolated incidents and short-lived, whereas bad stuff is viewed as all-encompassing and long-lasting.

Your perception about why something is happening to you can be the difference between starting to heal and preventing healing. When I used to feel hard done by and sorry for myself, I'd give myself a hard time for scratching, and even when my boyfriend told me that I was more than my skin, that my personality and eyes were attractive to him, regardless of what else was going on, I thought he was wrong and that nobody would ever really find me attractive.

When I fell into that hopeless mindset, I'd feel useless. I would see my eczema as a problem that I would always have, and because I'd been told this was a life-long condition that would never heal, it was not surprising I felt this sense of permanence. Then, when the periods of healthy skin I experienced didn't last, this pessimistic perception became a self-fulfilling prophecy and proved me right. During those days where I would sink down into self-pity, I feared I would never get better, and would always have to suffer this terrible condition.

Thankfully, my explanatory style wasn't 100% pessimistic, and, the good news is, even the most hardened pessimist can become more optimistic. I've always been a driven person so, despite those downward negative spirals, I didn't intend to give up. I realised that successful periods of clear skin were sometimes down to me and how I ate and exercised – but I still attributed a lot of it to external causes, such as the warmer climate, rather than internal reasons, such as how I felt and responded and what I thought about.

That small slice of optimism – of seeing that some of what I did could sometimes make a small difference – helped prevent me from giving up. I would tell myself if I tried harder to find a solution, perhaps I would. Even the tiniest amount of hope can be enough to help you cope.

That glimmer of hope spurred me on. I knew that diet and exercise and skincare helped. But they didn't heal me for long enough. My skin was still only temporarily clear and my eczema would still flare up from time to time, even when I was eating healthily and exercising sufficiently.

Something was missing; a special healing ingredient. But what could it be?

california dreamin'

I first realised my mind had an impact on my eczema when I was studying abroad in California and started reading the book *You Can Heal Your Life,* by Louise Hay. In the book she spoke about how she believed different ailments could be healed with a change in your mindset and through the use of positive affirmations. She had healed herself in this way, and lived to the ripe old age of 90.

I only half believed her until I saw the effects for myself.

In California I was happy, thriving in the sunshine and thinking positive thoughts. However, I failed to realise at the time what an impact my happy mind made to my skin. I was convinced I thrived in the heat of the beautiful sunshine, not that my 'mind' was happier in the sunshine.

When I returned to the UK I was sad to leave my friends and I lost my sense of belonging. I was looking for a home to live in, whilst securing my work internship and travelling all over the place without feeling like I had a 'base'. My lifestyle completely changed. This lack of belonging negatively impacted my mind, and therefore my skin. Of course, I didn't realise this at the time. I just blamed the gloomy weather and English culture.

It wasn't until I hit rock bottom that the evidence to support the notion of happy mind/happy skin began to accumulate.

mind matters

When I came out of hospital, I was in a very negative state of mind. I felt so sorry for myself and couldn't see any positives in my situation. I still refused to let the eczema win, though, and would go running fuelled by green juice.

However, my mother wouldn't stand for such negativity, and instinctively knew something deeper was going on and that my mind could do with some sort of 'healing'. She encouraged me to think 10 positive thoughts daily and to write them down. I found this very tough and a bit ridiculous at the time. But she persisted, as caring mothers do, and encouraged me to see an NLP (Neuro-Linguistic Programming) coach.

NLP is a personal development communication approach grounded in psychotherapy, which can help you to shift the way you think, the way you perceive past events and the way you approach life. It really boils down to shifting how you perceive things. The 'linguistic' part refers to the type of language you use to influence brain behaviour (the 'neuro' part) and recode (the 'programming' part) how your brain responds. In doing so it can help you respond better in the future and perceive past events in a more positive way too.

I didn't like the idea at first. I thought I was a strong-willed person, and it kept frustrating me that people thought changing my mindset would help. But she rang an NLP practitioner, pushed the phone onto me and the practitioner managed to convince me into having one session with him.

Seeing the NLP coach was a turning point in my life; one of the most transformative steps I took. The NLP coach helped reduce my worries and turn my negative thoughts into positive ones. I felt as if a weight had been lifted off my shoulders in just one session. I began to sleep better, without waking up in distress, scratching. He helped me see light at the end of my journey and was a huge part of my healing. That was the beginning of me thinking positively again, and the start of my healing journey. To find a practitioner near you, visit anlp.org.

This experience was so valuable. It made me realise I can control my life instead of life controlling me. It empowered me to think that a shift in mindset can be your greatest asset in keeping eczema away.

After noticing the impact my positive mindset made on my skin and realising how much our state of mind matters, I reflected on my life so far. I've kept a journal of when my skin has been at its worst and when it's been at its best, and I can safely say, during periods of my life when my positivity levels have been at their maximum, my eczema has been at its minimum.

Whenever I've felt good, whenever I've felt happiest, my skin has been at its clearest.

I went from covering my hands with gloves and my skin with make-up at high school, where I wasn't as happy, to a having a lot less eczema when I was in a happy routine at boarding school.

When I studied in California, I was at my most positive and my skin glowed with health. I was so proud of myself for taking a leap of faith to travel so far on my own at the age of 20. It gave me a huge sense of achievement and pride. I believed in my skills and confidence, and I saw a very bright future for myself. I was blissfully unaware of the challenges I would face on my return to the UK.

When I became a raw chef and took a road trip to France, I was in a positive state of mind, and so my eczema was minimal.

The next time I was this optimistic was when I began studying to become a health coach. After an awful five years post-California, I finally felt on track with my purpose in life again. This gave me the confidence to start writing my book, sharing my story and putting me on the path to where I am today.

Having gathered all of this evidence from living it, I realised how positive thoughts have the power to make the body thrive, while, conversely, negative ones can bring down the immune system.

Indeed, when I discovered the power of shifting my mindset to become more positive, I began to truly heal. Of course, it is not always easy to think positively, but trying to do so as much as possible is absolutely vital if you want to live a healthy life and heal your skin.

I can't deny that some days I still get tired, stressed and fall into a negative thinking pattern. The difference is that now I understand the huge impact it makes to my skin, I have taught myself to quickly snap out of it, and I use my own HOPE Principles to help me. I believe I will gain nothing from thinking negatively, but I can gain lots from thinking positively.

It makes sense that the better you feel inside, the better you look outside. But what about cultivating an optimistic state when life is really hard? When circumstances beyond your control are getting you down? How do you stay positive when everything around you is negative?

It took me a decade to figure this one out, but I've realised that's when you need to ramp up the self-care and self-compassion, and take care of yourself by:

- **being grateful**: looking for what's good in your life and documenting it;
- **getting calm**: finding time to meditate mindfully and just breathe;
- **getting out and being active**: being in nature by doing as much outdoor exercise as you can.

Sometimes taking good care of yourself is as simple as acknowledging you are thinking negatively, accepting that is the way you feel, and thinking about how you can help yourself to feel better right now. Maybe you need an early night? A walk in nature (after all, positive motion creates positive emotion)? Some time to meditate? Or perhaps listing all that you have to feel grateful for will shift your mind towards a brighter mood?

All of these things will help you feel better and cope better.

We've already explored how to get calm in Chapter 6, and we'll explore getting out and about in nature and being active in Chapter 10 (Eating Well, Exercise and Ecotherapy). For now, let's focus on the first of these ways to stay positive, a key contributor to the Optimism of O – gratitude.

an attitude of gratitude

I've cultivated a daily and weekly gratitude practice, and have started to use affirmations and visualisations, which were introduced to me when I first met a NLP practitioner.

When you focus on what is good now (gratitude and 'I am' affirmations), and what you hope will be good in the future (visualisation), you can let go of past troubles and focus on finding and expressing all the good stuff. Developing an attitude of gratitude in this way helps you to count your blessings rather than focus on your flaws.

Gratitude is a simple way to rewire our natural negative wiring towards appreciation; some studies have proven that it has more of an impact on depression than anti-depressants. It can even help improve sleep. Most of all, it can take us from that oh-so-common downward spiral into an upward one.

All we need to do is tune our minds into paying more attention to things, experiences, people, places, moments, memories, actions and words that bring us joy. When we set ourselves the daily task of looking for stuff to be grateful for, we are more likely to find it. And just the process of seeking stuff to appreciate makes it easier to cultivate gratitude as a long-lasting attitude.

It's important to express and/or record that gratitude in some way too. You might choose to do this by writing in a journal that you set aside as a special gratitude journal, every day when you wake or before you go to sleep. You could do this on a weekly basis instead. I find Sunday nights work well for gratitude journaling, as you can cast your mind back over the week that's gone and reflect. If I forget on a Sunday night, I make sure I do this on a Monday morning, as expressing gratitude is probably the best way to start a week. It definitely sets you off on the right foot.

Sometimes, for really special moments, experiences and gratitude-worthy stuff, I try to stay with the feeling of gratitude for as long as I can; to savour it. And I say 'thank you' a lot more than I ever did. Our parents teach us to say 'thank you' when we are children. They want us to be polite. But saying thank you to people and really feeling deep gratitude for what they have said or done can be really powerful. It not only connects you to the person you are thanking, it also connects you to your own attitude of gratitude and maximises it.

I create photo books and printed collages featuring photos of people or moments I'm deeply grateful for. I keep these on my bookshelf, and display them on my wall to serve as a constant reminder of all I have to be grateful for. Then, whenever I feel a bit down and need to get into a more positive mindset, I just open my photo book, or look at my collage, and reflect with gratitude on the subjects of the photographs. It's a great way to collect everything I'm grateful for in one place.

Another less 'hands-on' option could be to have a 'gratitude album' on your phone where you save photos of people or moments. Either way, it's really helpful to collect images which spark feelings of gratitude in you whenever you look at them.

The longer you can savour these feelings of gratitude, the better. Savouring involves really feeling the gratitude in your body as well as in your head. Savouring helps commit those good experiences to memory. I found out that our brains, given that they are predisposed to seeking out and responding to danger, tend to commit more negative experiences to memory than positive ones. It's the brain's way of protecting us (if we can remember everything that threatens us, we can stay safe). That's why we need to give our brains a bit of a nudge towards storing all the good stuff too.

I like to schedule in time to read my gratitude journal every month or so; to remind me on a constant basis of what is right, rather than (like I used to do) devoting so much time to focusing on what is wrong.

affirmations and re-framing

There is a great deal of power in affirming something positive to yourself, as we explored in the section on mindfulness in Chapter Six. Additionally, as well as looking at ourselves in the mirror while we affirm positive and encouraging statements, it's important to look at ourselves through a lens of compassion and approval. It's important to accept and even celebrate imperfection and vulnerability, and to know that you are enough. It's all too easy to give ourselves a hard time and beat ourselves up, but life can be tough enough without our own internal judgements and negative chatter adding to it.

Sometimes we believe the negative thoughts we tell ourselves, even if we don't have any evidence to support those thoughts. Sometimes our beliefs about ourselves are outdated – for example, that we'll never succeed or heal or change – but we'll never know if we don't try. So often when we say we can't do something, that becomes our truth. It's always far better to try and fail than to never try, because, as I've learned, even if we fail we learn something we didn't know before we tried. It's all useful, especially when it comes to healing, which is often a process of trial and error.

And, talking of errors. It's a shame to be self-critical based on beliefs or thoughts that aren't accurate and are laden with errors. That's why re-framing is so important.

Going back to the brain science again – thanks to something called neuro-plasticity, we are able to replace inaccurate thoughts which don't serve us with accurate ones that do. Our thoughts create neural pathways, which become beliefs. In order to carve out new, more helpful and realistic beliefs about ourselves and our abilities and our worth, we can think different thoughts.

Replacing thoughts with new ones is certainly easier than stopping yourself from thinking a negative thought. When you catch yourself thinking a negative thought, you can either try to stop thinking it or try to replace it with a new one, so it will create a new neural pathway and belief system. Not thinking a thought is a difficult ask, because we can't really tell ourselves not to think about something. As soon as we do, that's all we can think about! We can distract ourselves with gratitude and actions that will generate more positive emotions, but, on the whole, we really need to try to replace a thought rather than stop it.

The best way to do this is to question the thought. For example: am I really never going to heal? What if I could find a way? What if I could find someone else who has done so by reading books, chatting on forums and trying things out? I have a good chance of figuring out a solution if I apply myself. I've achieved goals before, so there's a chance that I can achieve this goal of healing. Yes, I can do this.

Replacing self-defeating and self-critical thoughts with ones that are based on facts, past achievements and future possibilities can help you carve out a positive mindset. Especially if you take those positive thoughts and affirm them on a regular basis:

- I am healed.
- I am well.
- I am loved.

Your turn. Try it. Go and find a mirror and create your new truth.

visualisation

Another optimism tool to pop into your healing toolkit is visualisation. This is when you picture, in your mind's eye, your desired future. See yourself healed, doing everything you want to do, with the people you want to be doing it with, being your best self. Picture all the details and daydream about it as if it's happened; as if this is your life now. Imagine sharing your story of how you healed and how you achieved your dreams. Hear yourself explaining what you've done, and how life is for you now. See it, feel it, believe it.

You can go one step further and create a vision board. I try to make one every year – a vision of what I desire and hope for in my life – pictures of me at my healthiest, pictures of places I wish to visit, pictures of a healthy lifestyle. All surrounded with quotes and words and images which inspire and motivate me.

Gratitude, affirmations and visualisation are a powerful combination to help you feel appreciative of the life you have and hopeful about the life you desire. These methods can boost your mindset to enable you to respond better to whatever happens on the roller-coaster journey of life.

reaction is better than cure

Life doesn't always go the way you plan but I believe it is generally for our greatest good. How we respond to what happens to us is vital to living a healthy and happy life:

We can choose how to react:

- We can choose to regret stuff we've done or said, or resent others or ourselves for our actions, or we can choose to learn from mistakes and forgive others and ourselves for our actions.
- We can choose to list everything that's wrong, or list everything that's right.
- We can choose a grumpy response, or a grateful response.

This isn't about glossing over the stuff that seems to be going wrong in our lives. It's about noticing both negative and positive situations, but investing time to savour the good and recognising that, sometimes, even the most difficult challenges can bring rewards and lessons and behaviours, which can only be seen as positive.

If I had never had eczema, I wouldn't have learned all of this juicy scientific information about boosting my own wellbeing, so that I could help others to do so too. I would likely also still be eating a whole lot of unhealthy food and feeling a lack of energy rather than buzzing with it. I may well be languishing rather than flourishing. And I certainly wouldn't even have looked into the option of studying abroad.

My eczema was the thought process for that adventure. So I'm grateful to all the adversity for gifting me this knowledge, those decisions and these life-enhancing practices, which I simply wouldn't know about or have stepped into, had it not been for my eczema journey.

It took me a long time to get over my eczema consuming my entire body. It totally broke my heart, and sometimes I wonder why it happened. But then I say to myself "You went through this to realise just how strong you are, and now you have come out the other side, you can provide hope to others."

A positive mindset has helped me feel powerful rather than feel like a victim.

A positive mindset gave me the power back over my life and eczema journey.

So here I am, sharing these practical ways that I have cultivated a more optimistic approach to my future, so you can apply them to your life and bring more optimism and hope into yours.

"And the time came when the risk to remain tight in a bud was more painful than the risk it took to blossom."

ANAIS NIN

CHAPTER 8

P is for Purpose

Having a purpose in life is so important. Whether that purpose is pursuing a career in a certain industry, or being a mother, or father, or being of service in some way, everyone needs something that they are excited about in life; something to which they feel called, compelled or curious enough to do.

When you are driven to live a purposeful life, it not only takes your mind off the suffering that eczema causes, it can also help reduce the amount of eczema you get. I've found that the more I've shown up to carve out a life that I love, the less eczema I get.

The bottom line is, when you show up, eczema doesn't (or certainly not as much).

When I found out that "meaning" is another of the six pillars of wellbeing (according to positive psychology experts), it didn't surprise me. After all, it's only since I've truly felt like my life has meaning that I've truly flourished. When you feel aimless rather than purposeful, that's when you are more likely to struggle mentally. And, when I struggle mentally, the evidence makes itself known on my skin with an eczema flare-up.

I now truly believe that one of the reasons I struggled for so long with my eczema was because I felt a bit lost and jaded career-wise. Apart from a few times, such as my time living in California, I wasn't living a life that felt worthwhile or had meaning in terms of being aligned to my hopes and dreams. I had an incredibly strong vision of what I wanted, but I kept losing sight of how to get there. I had always known I was drawn to the natural health industry, but my forays into it hadn't worked out as I'd hoped; hence this feeling of lack when it came to meaning.

I would try to make things happen, but came up against so many obstacles. I kept getting knocked back over and over. I'd lost my internship because of my skin condition, and I hadn't been able to find paying work that could sustain me, so I'd had to work for my dad, which made me feel like I'd let everyone down, even though my dad insisted I was an invaluable asset to his business. And, although I appreciated the opportunity to earn money and learn so much about the business, I wasn't doing work which I felt was my true calling.

So I felt aimless, like I wasn't in control or in command of my life. Rather, life circumstances and my eczema were in the driving seat. I was trying to show up, but couldn't fully because I lacked belief in and control of my situation.

It took me a long time to figure out that "Purpose" was indeed part of the healing puzzle. Now I realise that having a purpose when you wake up each morning is such a motivator, and I've found it integral to my own healing journey.

Thankfully, my trip to Australia taught me that pursuing a career in the health and wellness industry was possible and gave me the motivation to try again – but this time I would put myself in the driving seat.

Sometimes that's all it takes – one light bulb moment where you see other people doing what you want to do, and you realise that anything is possible. When one door closes, another one often opens, even if it takes a while for that to happen.

There are many routes towards finding meaning, towards pursuing what matters most to you. Living a purposeful life requires effort and determination, a good dose of self-awareness and knowledge of what you love to do and what you're good at, but it also requires enough grit that you can pivot and change course if one route isn't taking you towards that desired destination.

I've learned that the hard way – with all those obstacles en route – but I got there in the end! And every obstacle taught me something. Every adversity I've endured or mistake I've made has provided insightful lessons.

For example, from my first internship I learned not to put your hopes and dreams into the hands of one person, or anyone that is not you. I also learned from my time at university that you can only steer yourself in the right direction when you're in the driving seat. I had done the courses that were expected of me, rather than the courses I felt fascinated by. I had left my destiny under other people's control, rather than seizing control myself.

And that is what my travels in Australia taught me – that I was fully responsible for choosing what to do with my life.

It was up to me.

Consequently what changed, for me, was my decision to try to take control of my life by saving up to do a course that excited me and fitted with my true passion for health and wellness.

I'd always been really passionate about health and fitness, travelling and working out. When I was young I thought I wanted to be a model, but then I realised it was the model's lifestyle which appealed to me, rather than the job of modelling. I love that models got to travel and experience different parts of the world and I loved the art and creativity of modelling. If I could work in an industry which enabled me to live that way of life, I'd live an aligned life. But if I could do that while making a difference to others too, that'd be my dream; that would give my life meaning and purpose.

I thought, when I left school, I could be a beautician or personal trainer, but I really wasn't sure. My dad (who I admire for what he has achieved in business) was keen for me to go to university, so that's what I did. But I couldn't keep away from nutrition. I was so drawn to it that while I was studying marketing at uni, I'd spend each night reading nutrition books, like the nerd I am. Whenever I got a chance I read nutrition and fitness books/magazines and practically lived in the organic shop down the road. In fact, this is the shop that really connected me with my best friend Ashley. She was studying abroad from Canada and we bonded over our mutual love of natural food and health products.

These were the clues that life offered up to me about what I was most passionate about. But I still needed to go on a journey of discovery to figure out what I truly did (and didn't) desire. And therein lies the key to finding your purpose – you need to gain experience of the good, the bad and the downright un-purposeful to know what matters most to you.

the purpose treasure hunt

Yes, I've definitely found, you need to do something you DON'T love in order to find out what you DO love – or, vice versa, do something in an industry you DO love in order to find out what you DON'T love about it. These twists and turns in the road will take you onto your truest path. You may already know what you love to do, what would give your life the most meaning, but you may not be aware of the parts of those tasks, and roles and areas of life within it, that you enjoy less.

For example, my whole family is into business, in the property market in particular. However, working in an office within that industry isn't particularly creative. As a creative and active person, I couldn't get into that work environment or role. I DIDN'T love working there, so I tried to gain experience in an industry I DID love – the health industry.

I love learning about the body, how it works, I love art and sport and I knew working in the health industry would mean learning more about something I was driven by. But it was only through working in that industry, which I DID love, that I learned that marketing – even for a health company – is very business-oriented, and involves spending a lot of time in an office on the computer.

So, by working in a space that I DID love, I learned what I DIDN'T love. I learned that, whatever I did, I wanted to create and build and make stuff, and if I did need to do anything computer related, then I'd rather work from a café in my gym clothes, rather than in an office environment wearing smart clothes. I DID love doing the former but DIDN'T love the latter.

As I discovered when I moved home and worked for the family business after my degree, working in an office wasn't great for my skin, nor was the property industry I was working in, because I truly wasn't living my passions.

I DID enjoy working in the juice bar as I got to make food, and loved the creativity of doing that and working for a business in the health sector. I also furthered my passion for pursuing a career that would do good and have a positive effect on those I served.

So, when I did finally take control over my career, I focused on carving out something where I could make and build stuff– content, creams, books and dreams – something where I could make a difference to people's lives in the process.

That is what I'm doing with www.thebeautyofeczema.com now.

living a purposeful life

Of course, living purposefully – living a life with meaning – doesn't have to be about what you do for a living. It can be about what you spend your time doing in other ways. For example, motherhood and fatherhood are purposeful roles in life – children can give our lives meaning. So can hobbies and other pursuits.

Living a purposeful life gives you a sense of belonging, as you feel you share common values with others who share your passion, and it can also help you feel needed. For example, if your purpose in life is to be a parent, to bring up your child or children, to be part of a family, or to provide for that family, to whom you teach your values – you are needed. Your life has meaning.

Or perhaps that meaning comes from being part of a movement or living your life a certain way. For example, living healthily, being green and ethical; those values foster a sense of belonging and give meaning to your life as you do your bit to save the planet.

If you think that your purpose and sense of meaning will come mainly from the type of work you do, as is the case for me, it can be draining when you feel that your hands are tied, that you simply cannot pursue your passion immediately – due to financial constraints or time constraints, due to responsibilities you may have or simply because you love your job, even if it's not especially purposeful.

Of course, you may be in a job that isn't especially purposeful, but it might be fun to work at your workplace. Perhaps being there makes you feel good and you love being around the people you work with. Perhaps it gives you a good sense of belonging and/or a solid opportunity to grow and progress. You may even be using your strengths to undertake the job you're doing.

If so, that's awesome, because it's important to love what you do and enjoy going to work. It's also meaningful to do work where you use your strengths. There's no point leaving a job that makes you feel good, just because it isn't your true 'calling' or because it doesn't feel especially meaningful. There are plenty of other ways to pursue your purpose. And your job could provide you with more meaning than you realise, especially if you feel comfortable in the role you're in.

In these instances, you can:

1. Stay in your job, but pursue your passions through voluntary work or in your spare time or
2. Seek out ways to at least try to overcome financial or time constraints by figuring out ways to earn or save more money, and to optimise your time (for example, by seeing friends while exercising or cycling to work, to give you back time spent at the gym) – so you can use that saved time to do more of what you love.
3. Consider what else might be stopping you. Fear? Expectations? Beliefs? Lack of belief?

what's stopping you?

Fear is the biggest enemy of cultivating a meaningful life. Fear, along with perceived lack of money or time.

Perhaps you think you just don't have enough time or money to retrain or to take a certain course.

Perhaps you fear failure. What if it doesn't work out and you've wasted all that time or proved everyone who said you couldn't do it right? Or, what if it does work out and you prove everyone wrong?

Perhaps someone else (or someone else's expectations) are preventing you from pursuing your passions. Your partner or a family member might be holding you back by telling you that you can't or shouldn't do something. Maybe the fear comes from your fear of letting people down?

I'll cut to the chase – it took me a long time to realise, but if any of these ring true for you, the only person standing in your way is you! Just as I was letting my own fears (of measuring up, or letting people down, or being good enough) stand in my way.

You see, deep down, I always wanted to be part of the health, fitness and beauty industry but I kept telling myself I couldn't. Either I couldn't afford it, thought I wasn't good enough, healthy-looking enough, or felt that my eczema was standing in my way, just because it had felt that way when I lost my internship as a direct result of my skin condition.

I fed myself endless excuses about why I couldn't.

'I can't' became my story.

I had always been a driven person, but the knock-backs and my eczema had really knocked my confidence.

I told myself that I'd tried, but it hadn't worked out. I also told myself that if I ever gained control over my skin, I would write a book about it. But I kept putting that off too. I just kept saying, 'I can't. I'm not a good enough writer.'

The good news is, there are always ways round a brick wall. You can climb over it or go round it, but there's always a way around what's blocking you. For example, I eventually found someone to help me with my book. As soon as I replaced 'I can't' with 'How can I?', I discovered my pathway towards living a purposeful life.

So, think about it. What if you replaced 'I can't' with 'How can I?' What difference would that make to you living a purposeful life?

For example:

- How can I spend more time being creative?
- How can I write a book?
- How can I take tiny steps towards retraining?

For me, 'I can't become a health coach' became, 'how can I become a health coach?' My answer to that question was by saving up enough money to do the qualification.

As soon as I realised fear was holding me back and realised 'if they can, I can', there was a huge shift in how I perceived and approached my office work for my dad:

- I saw working for my dad as a platform.
- It became the route towards my dreams.
- It made me willing to continue working in order to fund a dream I WAS super passionate about.

I also sought out additional streams of income by selling stuff I no longer needed at a local market.

I did whatever I could to make my dreams come true.

For me, 'I can't write a book' became 'I *can* write a book, but I'm going to need some help'. I found a way to make it happen and I found a wonderful lady who could work with me to create this very book that you're now reading. Writing this book has been done through interviews, transcripts, my old diaries and numerous questions until the book I was trying to create was formed. Chapter by chapter I saw my vision becoming a reality! I found a way round the brick walls, and you can too.

Most importantly, I took action. And that's how you can break through whatever is holding you back.

However, it's important to say, it took me a couple of years to find the courage to do so – to take the first step in the direction of creating my dream life. I first looked into the Institute of Integrative Nutrition course over the summer of 2013, when I finished my internship. Polly Noble had taken the course, and lots of respected wellness gurus had too. The problem was, I didn't have the money to cover the cost of the course at the time, and I still had to finish my marketing degree.

It wasn't until I found out my friend in Australia had done it and was living her dream life that I considered it once more. Yet, I have to admit, even then, even once I'd made the decision to save up to pay for it and even when I had finally saved enough to sign up, my head still filled with doubts.

I almost let fear make the decision for me and stop me from signing up. I remember feeling scared about whether my investment would pay off and whether I should spend all this money on this course, or just carry on saving. Then I started to question my abilities. Am I really going to be a good health coach? Am I healthy enough to be a health coach?

Enrolment was literally going to close in a few hours, and I left it right until the last minute because fear had taken control. Thankfully, I listened to my strong gut feeling rather than the voices of my inner critic and fear inside my head. I knew I had to follow my heart. So, I called up and put my deposit for the course down.

i'd done it – I'd taken that crucial first step. And do you know what? Once you've taken that first step, the rest flows so much more easily. The course was online, so I wasn't hemmed in by the location. I could fit the course flexibly around me. Doing this course was the best decision I've ever made, and one where I listened to my own heart and followed it, rather than listening to the advice of others. It was all down to me, and that felt good. I was back in the driving seat of my life.

I want the same for you.

Once I'd taken that first step, there was no stopping me. During the last month of my health coaching diploma, I signed up to do the natural chef diploma course. Food and mood are a huge part of wellness, so it was important to me to study and gain qualifications in both areas.

And I've thoroughly enjoyed the process of running through nutrition slides, cooking and taste-testing foods, recreating my own version of the dishes at home and writing up the health benefits of the recipes.

Right now, I'm in my element and loving it. But none of this would have happened if I'd settled for an office-based working life, or if I'd let my fear talk me out of taking action.

What's more, something else taking intentional action towards my dreams gave me was confidence that I've got my own back; that

I can do what's right for me. I'd made the right decision and I'd made it myself. I could do this after all.

As soon as you start realising and believing that you can do this, it becomes a self-fulfilling prophecy as you prove yourself right (just as is the case when you tell yourself you can't, because then you don't).

meaning boosts wellbeing

The impact that living a purposeful life has had on me, my skin and my wellbeing has been tremendous. Little did I know the difference having something meaningful to do would have on my own confidence and sense of purpose. Making a difference to others has made a difference to me. I'm using my strengths and skills to do something I feel incredibly passionate about.

As a direct result of this, I feel more at ease, more aligned and more 'at home' than I've ever felt and my eczema is practically non-existent, because all the puzzle pieces are working together.

Studies back up why my wellbeing has been boosted, as research shows that commitment to a purpose makes it easier to be optimistic and overcome obstacles. We are better able to persist through challenges when we have a clear direction. It makes sense – if you're going on a journey and you have a clear sense of where you are headed, you're much more likely to get back on your bike if you get knocked off.

Cheryl Rickman says in her *Flourish Handbook*, "When we find a way to link our experiences into a meaningful pattern, we feel more in control of our life. Conversely when life feels random and aimless, we feel more out of control and, studies show, less happy."

It's comforting to have a sense of direction, and that's what living a purposeful life provides – it gives life meaning and directionality. If we are going somewhere, we are growing somehow, rather than being stagnant. And it feels good to grow, just as it feels good to work towards something. Yes, it's reassuring to have a strong idea about where we are headed, and why.

That tiny act of signing up to the health coach course was the first step towards creating a meaningful life with purpose. No matter how small that tiny act of devotion towards your dreams is, it matters.

So what's it going to be?

What can you start to see as a platform rather than a prison?

How can you make it happen for yourself?

I've learned there are two stages to this.

1. Self-awareness. Know what you want, what matters most to you. Get to know yourself.
2. Self-belief. Replace 'I can't' with 'How can I? Then formulate a plan – a route map that will help you reach your destination – and visualise yourself living your purposeful life.

purpose quiz: getting to know you and what matters most

"It's never too late to be what you might have been,"

George Eliot

Knowing what your values are about means knowing what matters most to you. That's an integral part of living a purposeful life, because only when you know who you are and what matters most to you can you live an aligned and authentic life with meaning.

Imagine yourself old and frail and looking back on your life. Imagine yourself saying you wish you'd done this, that or the other, or that you wish you'd been kinder, braver, friendlier. It's unlikely that you'd wish you'd accumulated more material items. You'd regret not doing or not being, rather than not buying. Consider what you'd wish you had done or been.

The answers to this question show you what is important to you, what matters most to you and what doesn't. It flags up your value system and the things you would love to do.

Other questions to help you increase your self-awareness around what matters most include:

- What do you hope to achieve in life? If you had a magic wand – where would you see yourself in one year's time? Five years' time?

- What are you grateful for about your life already, as it is now?
- What makes you feel fuzzy, joyful and excites you when you do it?
- If you had to make a list of five activities that nourish you, what would you write?
- What did you used to love doing when you were 10?
- What and who and where inspires you? Activities, people, places?
- Which achievements are you most proud of?
- What makes you most proud to be you?
- Which problems bother you most in the world, that you'd most like to see solved? Which causes do you care most about?
- What would you do if you knew you couldn't fail (or, if you did fail, it wouldn't matter because you love doing it regardless of how successful you are at it)?
- What are your superpowers – your main three strengths (imagine someone else was describing you, what would they say)? For example, it might be creativity, kindness or being organised.
- What comes easily to you? What do you feel right doing and enjoy doing? For example, writing, drawing, calming people down, encouraging people? If your friends could hire you to do one thing for them, what would it be? Style them with a whole new wardrobe? Sort their garden out? Help them get fitter or healthier? Give them encouraging pep talks when they're doubting themselves?
- What do you find yourself wishing for? More money? Better health? Slimmer waistline? All of the above? If so, which is the priority, and why?

- How could you use your talents and your passion to make a difference?
- Which values do you hold dear?
- How do you wish to be seen, and how would you hope to be remembered?
- Do you feel 'called' to do something in particular?
- Are you living up to your own expectations? What are those, and why? Are they realistic?
- What would you need to do in order to reach your potential? What's getting in the way?
- When have you been helpful to others? How did you help? You may take for granted the strengths that feel like common sense to you, but are useful to others.
- What could you teach others?

plot your route map

Living with purpose means that your hopes are aligned with your actions. Once you know what you want to do and achieve – ie where your destination is – you need to create a routemap so you know how to get there. That's basically a plan filled with intentional actions. Your actions can now flow from your answers to the above questions. You can use what you've written to map out a plan of action filled with intentions to help you live a more purposeful, meaningful life.

You might love visiting bookstores and reading snippets and buying a selection of books. If so, perhaps you could work or volunteer in a bookstore from time to time or carve out time to visit bookstores more often. Perhaps you feel all fuzzy when you make children laugh or when you entertain your friends. Could you figure out ways to do this more often? Perhaps you come into your own when you give advice, send out support packages or speak up for someone in need. Does your career give you the opportunity to do this, or is it something you could volunteer to do more of? Making a meal and sitting down with loved ones to enjoy it might spark a sense of joy inside you. If so, how might you do more of that?

If you are thinking of starting your own business or going freelance, you need to be passionate about whatever area you intend to work in. You need to be passionate and enthusiastic about it, because it's incredibly hard being your own boss. And passion keeps you going when the going gets tough.

As soon as I decided to become a health coach, I thought about my business every single day. I would write Post-it notes about everything I wanted to achieve and share with the world, and I'd stick them up on my laptop screen, my fridge at home, anywhere I regularly looked. I would tell myself every day and night what I was aiming for, and express it to friends. I had a dream, a plan, and no matter how silly people thought my ideas were, I wasn't going to give up.

visualise it

Alongside your routemap, I also recommend seeing your destination in your mind's eye. Seeing your vision becoming a reality can be really powerful. Imagining yourself telling people all about how you got where you are helps too.

Once I had a routemap, I also created a vision board with a section on saving money, a section on becoming an entrepreneur, having a lifestyle I could work from anywhere, a section on having 10/10 health, love, being close to my family and living a beach lifestyle. This vision board served as a reminder about what appealed most, mattered most and would drive me most on my journey to getting where I wanted to be – to living a life with purpose and meaning.

keep going

Sometimes I have to pinch myself that I am actually living and working on my dream business. I take one day at a time, and I am loving the process.

Nowadays there is no such thing for me as a typical day, because every day is different. I get to wear so many different hats as a health coach, natural chef, entrepreneur and author. If I'd known then what I know now, I wouldn't have wasted so much of my precious time worrying about the future.

Today I'm living my dream and mostly eczema-free. But it hasn't been easy arriving at this dream destination. And I certainly don't ever rest on my laurels or get complacent about my achievements. I still work incredibly hard – in fact, harder than I've ever worked before.

When I am wearing my chef hat, I have had intern hours to complete. I've done 40 hours in a local café and did 60 hours cheffing on a retreat in Tuscany for around 30 guests. That experience was incredible and, as it coincided with writing the final chapters of my book, it's provided me with proof that living a creative life, where I cook nourishing food for myself and others, provides me with the meaning that fuels my sense of wellbeing.

Every other week I commuted to London for my chef class, where I'd spend a whole day learning the nutrition of certain foods, how to cook them and how to add them to certain dishes. I've completed assignments on recipe development and testing, have written therapeutic meal plans for various ailments, and have written a business plan too.

For my exam I had to cook for 20 people and run the entire event with my colleagues. I was in charge of desserts, decorations and photography, skills that I'm excited about incorporating into my purposeful work, by writing my own recipes on a consistent basis and sharing them on my blog and via my YouTube channel.

When I wore my health coaching hat, I had Skype calls with potential clients and created a personalised plan from food to optimism techniques to a list of skincare products I recommend.

I'm also building and promoting my business and setting up a website packed full of useful content and recipes, so I've been spending time with my web developers, writing content and mapping out and filming video content. I've also been busy trying to create the best multi-purpose moisturiser for eczema sufferers. This is still in the early stages, but I think it is so important since I moisturise every single day and would love to make one especially for eczema sufferers with all the ingredients I love to use on my skin.

I have made exercise part of my daily life, whether that's yoga, running or weight lifting, and I prioritise self-care each evening, as I'll have a bath to relax from the stresses of the day and drink a magnesium drink to calm me before bed. I use affirmations in the morning as I do my makeup, surround myself with supportive friends either via Skype or in person, and I eat a balanced mindful diet and listen to my body. I am in the process of building my dream business and I am working on moving to a warmer climate abroad.

All the puzzle pieces are fitting together nicely. Don't get me wrong, some days you just can't control what life throws at you, but thanks to these self-care tools, I feel confident in staying in control of my eczema.

I am always learning and working on becoming the best version of myself. That way I can be a better coach, a better friend, girlfriend and family member. And, so far so good.

My mum is incredibly proud to see me chasing and now living my dream and praises my determination, and my dad tells me every day he believes in me and to never give up. I remember telling him recently that without him, I couldn't be doing what I'm doing. His response was something I will never forget: "Camille, you could do this without me, it would just take you a little longer." I am lucky they are both are supporting me, as are my siblings and friends.

Having eczema destroyed my soul at one point in my life but now I am grateful for what happened because my story could have an impact on healing people all over the world; people like you.

So, although my journey was quite painful, I'm glad I came out the other end. Because, by sharing my story with others, I hope to stop people from having to go through that and to enable people with eczema to get clearer skin more quickly, without letting it get as bad as I did and ending up in hospital.

By applying the principles I've learned throughout this journey to your own life, you can get where you want to be much quicker. But, no matter what happens, you must always have hope.

have hope

Having hope is so important during times of struggle and that's why I have called the jigsaw puzzle pieces of living a predominantly eczema-free life, my HOPE Principles. They work for me and they could for you.

I love the word HOPE, as it refers to that spark of feeling good about the future and it motivates us into action towards us achieving whatever it is we hope for. Hope propels us on during the difficult days. For some, hope is all they've got, and that is huge compared to having nothing hopeful at all.

No matter how challenging life can get, there is always hope. Even that you might make a living from sharing your story of how bad things got, just as I am. I am so blessed to have found my purpose from something that negatively affected my life. It has led me to find a passion for health, cheffing, skincare, and being of service to others who have also been where I have been, those who have walked in my shoes.

Had I not suffered with eczema, I may have just settled for a 9-5 job and still be lost as to what my true purpose in life was. Thankfully, I get to live my days feeling like I am positively contributing to this world. And you can too.

"Rest and self-care are so important. When you take time to replenish your spirit, it allows you to serve others from the overflow. You cannot serve from an empty vessel."

ELEANOR BROWNN

CHAPTER 9

P is also for Pampering

self-care is healthcare

My health journey is a journey for life. I can't just decide not to bother following all that I have learnt. If I sacrifice my workouts or eating in a way which nourishes me, or if I don't keep check of my stress, or forgo my self-care routine, my eczema WILL return.

I read in Chloe Brotheridge's book *The Anxiety Solution* that people think 'self-care is a luxury'. But it's not. It is an absolute necessity in order to thrive.

I am always learning and working on becoming the best version of myself, so that I can grow and become a better coach, friend, girlfriend and family member. And, given that happiness is contagious, the happier I am, the happier those I spend time with will be. So I need to do all that I can to help me to flourish, and self-care comes high up on the list of ways to enable that.

So, while the dictionary definition of the word 'pamper' is "to give someone special treatment, making that person as comfortable as possible and giving them whatever they want", I think it's important to see 'special treatment' as a normal day-to-day way of treating yourself, because you are! Special, that is.

'Special treatment' implies that you only pamper yourself on special occasions, ie rarely rather than regularly. But you're special enough that pampering should be a *daily* event, not something that's reserved for special occasions. If I've learned anything throughout my eczema journey, it's that looking after myself is vital and should therefore be prioritised. Taking care of our body, mind and soul is something we need to do on a daily basis. So I'd like you to revisit how you view pampering – to see it as a necessity rather than a luxury.

my skincare story

I was drawn to the notion of caring for my skin, long before I even realised how important a part of my life doing so would become; long before I knew the pain my skin would cause me and long before I knew how integral the care of my skin would be to my life journey.

Ever since I was a little girl, I was fascinated watching my mother apply all her products. She was a beautician and I always looked up to her for beauty advice. We shared this passion together as I grew up. Booking spa treatments in together and investing in the latest product rather than the latest fashion item. We both believed taking care of ourselves was a better investment than an external item like a handbag. Don't get me wrong, I love fashion pieces, but skincare always comes first.

Growing up, each morning and night, I had to use steroid creams and an extremely thick emollient moisturiser prescribed by the doctors, because if your skin gets dry and cracked, you're more susceptible to your eczema coming back. I would take my creams everywhere, and panic if I didn't have them with me. I was embarrassed by the medical labels and packaging of the products and wished I could be like my friends with their fancy pink beautifully-perfumed products.

As a result of wanting to be like everyone else, I used all the fancy products, and then masked my flare-ups with my medicated creams in secret. If only there had been a medicated cream with fancy packaging which also smelled nice! I had spotted a gap in the market even then, without realising it.

As I got older and went to boarding school, I was determined to understand why my skin flared up while everyone else's didn't. When my mother took me for tests and I was given a list of foods to avoid, I was also given a list of chemicals in skincare products. Until then, the notion of chemicals affecting skin was alien to me, but, when I went to check the ingredients of my shampoo, conditioner, face wash, body wash, sure enough, every product I put on my skin contained those 'drying' chemicals.

Even the emollient prescribed by the doctors contained paraffin. That's when I decided to find a compromise. I would still take the doctor's advice of moisturising daily every morning and evening, but I'd use a natural moisturiser instead to allow my skin to breathe, naturally.

I instantly threw the rest of my beauty products into the bin and went on a mission with my mum to find chemical-free products I could use. Together we discovered the 'Dead Sea Spa' range, and I used all their products throughout boarding school. They weren't fancy and pink, but they were natural and soothed my skin, which felt like a winning discovery.

The same applied for my make-up and perfume. I ditched bags of make-up and started to wear less. As soon as I did that, my skin began to glow.

I couldn't get away from perfume being full of chemicals, so I chose to spray it onto my clothing rather than directly onto my skin.

But I remember back then thinking, I wish I could create my own product line for eczema sufferers; something fun and brightly packaged containing only natural ingredients. Something that smelt nice yet didn't look medicated. For a 17 year old that vision seemed like a crazy dream. But, like all of the best ideas, it did sow a seed in my mind.

At the end of boarding school when we were all applying for university, I had no idea what I wanted to be. I just wanted to be happy and kind, keep my eczema away and travel the world. Naively, since that plan doesn't make a living or support a family.

So, I followed in my family's footsteps and applied for business management at a bunch of universities. I actually applied to the spa management course in Derby, as I felt that would support my secret dream of creating my own products one day. However, as a young woman with no clue of the impact such decisions would make, I let fear and self-doubt make the decision for me and declined it. I also preferred the idea of living down south in the beautiful town of Bath, especially because of their natural bath springs history and the bath spa itself.

So off I went to study business management – to find I couldn't stand the classes, my eczema was returning, and I was skipping class to read nutrition books in my room. I was clearly on the wrong course, and after changing degree around four times I dropped out, feeling rather ashamed. However, looking back now, I am proud I listened to my heart rather than listening to the expectations of others.

Once I'd dropped out and moved home, I did a nail technician course, which fired up my passion for working in the health and beauty industry. I won the modelling competition for natural beauty brand, LoveLula and became the face of their company. It was my brother who said that if I was to put my face to anything, it would have to be something I believed in, and this looked like the perfect opportunity. He suggested I go for it, and even helped me choose the pictures to send in.

A couple of days later I was accepted and, in a couple of weeks, I was modelling for the brand. I had gone from feeling ashamed for dropping out of university to living my dream modelling for a natural products company.

And that is where I was exposed to a whole range of natural beauty brands. I learnt there were so many more products I could use on my skin, and even natural make-up too. It was a revelation and a dream come true.

I started to think that perhaps I should make my own range some day, but ignored that calling and continued on my way. It all seemed like too big a dream for little me to pursue at the time.

As part of the modelling competition prize, I was given a year's supply of products – this huge box containing natural makeup, body wash and moisturisers. I was in product heaven. So I started my new university course in Cheltenham with all these beautiful products, feeling like I could pamper myself from head to toe without any concern for reactions.

When I then went to California to do my second year, I had grown reliant on my products. I was extremely scared to use anything but my own. I wondered how I would cope in America. 'What if they don't sell the products I use?' I thought. 'What if I flare up?' I'd be so far from home, what would I do? I remember speaking to my friend Holly about this, and her response was "Camille, you are going to California, this is your opportunity to try so many more natural skincare products! Embrace it instead of fearing it!" And she was right.

That combination of support and self-care was already proving itself to be a winning combination.

I remember one of my first adventures in California was to find a natural food store which sold all natural products, including skincare. I remember the lady working there said I reminded her of the young Jessica Alba as she used to shop in there. Obviously I was incredibly flattered and then did some research on Jessica, only to find out she had launched her own product range of child-friendly natural products. And so that thought returned – I wonder if I might have my own range too one day?

Those big dreams were soon dashed as I returned from California and ended up in hospital for my eczema, looking and feeling the complete opposite of healthy. How could I create my own products if I couldn't even win the battle with eczema? Consequently, I developed a fear of all products – even water stung my skin.

As I lost trust in doctors, my health idols, I also lost trust in my products. I felt like I was the only person I could rely on, so I started to research how I could make products myself.

That's when I started to make my own toothpaste using coconut oil, salt and peppermint oil; my own cleanser out of oils; my own nourishing baths with salts and oatmeal and my own skin treatments with pure aloe vera. I even tried to make my own shampoo out of cider vinegar, (although that was not so successful).

My fear of chemicals continued, so I stopped dying my hair blonde. I just wanted to be totally pure and natural so I could stop living in pain with eczema.

Thankfully as I started to heal and after spending a summer in France, with lots of vitamin D, salty sea, and yoga, my skin was naturally glowing and hair lightened. I was feeling more myself again. As I let my friends in, my trust in the world started to come back and, with that, my trust in skincare products returned.

To be honest, it was getting a bit exhausting trying to make everything from scratch and I had missed the ease of just buying a product. So I went back to trialling different kinds of products and worrying less about every single ingredient. By now I had learned that stressing over my products was more toxic than the product itself.

Now, I absolutely LOVE trying different natural products, but I also don't obsess over being 'perfectly natural' as that wasn't good for my mental health. I have gone back to dying my hair blonde as I love doing this and have done it from quite a young age.

So now, I'm not against beauty treatments that aren't natural, as long as they don't affect my skin. I have my favourite natural perfumes I can use from Pacifica (which I still spray on my clothes instead of my skin, as it's habitual to do so). I still make my own cleanser, body oil, bath treatments and face masks but I also have a bunch of products I can turn to for the simple pleasure of pampering.

And, finally, I have begun to listen to that inner guidance which kept wondering about creating a range. Yes, I have decided to chase that dream I kept a secret, and I am now in the process of creating my own natural skincare for eczema suffers.

I can visualise those products now: something deeply nourishing but a total treat, with beautifully colourful packing, because we eczema sufferers deserve that! It's all so new, but, by the time you read this, it might be available on my website ready to buy or on the shelves of beauty stores.

I am no longer silencing my ambition, I am chasing it, and I encourage you to do the same. I was 17 when I had this dream, now 27 – that's a whole decade of not pursuing it. Now it's time I stepped up and followed my passion to have my own range of eczema-friendly but beautifully packaged products.

And, if you have a dream, I recommend you don't wait that long, because your inner voice will keep speaking up until you do something about it. Better to do it sooner than later, because following your dreams is a great way to boost your levels of wellbeing.

my self-care and skincare rituals and routines

As you can see from my own journey and values, self-care matters a great deal. For me, self-care is about caring for every part of me: mind, body and soul – so mood, skin and food all matter. What I put into my body and what I put onto my body matters. How much I sleep and how much I move matters. Whether I think primarily positive or negative thoughts matters. I need to care for myself.

My family and friends know me as the pamper queen. If I ever go missing whilst everyone else is watching a movie, they know I am most likely to be pampering in my room. If I've ever left a night out, I'm most likely pampering, if I'm not answering my phone – pampering. You get the gist. I LOVE pampering, and believe YOU should too. It is the biggest act of love you can give yourself, alongside giving yourself time to breathe, get calm and just be.

Often times, one follows the other. So a pampering routine will end in some mindful mediation, or I can even practice mindfulness and affirmations during my routine. Similarly, if I choose to meditate in the mornings, I'll follow up with a pampering session.

I also ensure that exercise is an integral part of my daily life, whether that's yoga, running or weight lifting. I eat a balanced diet and listen to my body. I use affirmations in the morning as I do my make-up. I surround myself with supportive friends either via Skype or in person.

Each morning and evening, self-care is a top priority, ahead of and following a busy day. So I have a morning and evening pamper routine, which I stick to.

My morning routine energises my body. This consists of a hot shower, with a quick blast of cold water at the end. I use all-natural products in the shower, and then I'll towel dry and moisturise myself head to toe. I literally sit on a towel loving every inch of my skin, and thanking it for being so strong. If it is flared, that is when I give it extra love instead of hatred (easily done), as those are the days you need to be strong and love yourself even more.

After moisturising I like to coat the soles of my feet in essential oils (I like wild orange oil). I then brush my teeth and use a tongue cleaner (if you haven't got one, you honestly should), then I dry my hair and get dressed in clothes that make me 'feel good'. I sometimes spend the day fresh-faced. Other days I'll use my natural make-up.

My evening routine relaxes my body. It's all about winding down. First, I'll have a soak in my 'skin remedy' bath with a handful of Dead Sea salts or Epsom salts, castor oil and a drop of lavender essential oil, to relax from the stresses of the day. Sometimes, for a fun twist, I'll add in my own natural colour from superfood powders and some flowers from the garden. I'll either bathe in silence or play a meditation or calming music.

Then I'll do my moisturising. I moisturise every night and put some essential oils on my feet (as long as there is no broken skin). As I moisturise and massage myself from head to toe, I do the same gratitude ritual that I do each morning, where I thank every inch of my skin. If I see a small eczema patch I will kiss it and thank it for showing my body needs to slow down. Some days I create my own natural facemask, other days I enjoy trialling facemasks from my favourite natural beauty brands.

Sometimes I'll do a mini yoga flow, say a few positive affirmations in the mirror, perhaps picking up an affirmation card and reading from that to create a comforting zone of positivity before bed. I'll then drink a magnesium drink to calm me, light some incense and read a book before drifting off to sleep.

On weekends I like to treat myself to getting my nails painted (even if my hands are flared up). I encourage you to go, and you will realise nobody cares as much as you do about the cuts. I get my hair coloured as another pamper treat. On my most stressful days, I invest in a full body massage.

I know I am fortunate that my skin is glowing now and I can enjoy these massages. If you are struggling with your eczema to the degree you can't have a massage, I can sympathise with you. But I gained control, and believe you will too if you follow the HOPE Principles laid out in this book – you'll be able to enjoy a full body massage some day soon.

All the puzzle pieces are fitting together nicely. Don't get me wrong, some days you just can't control what life throws at you, but, thanks to these self-care tools, I feel confident in staying in control of my eczema. I am now the boss of it, rather than it being the boss of me.

skincare secrets: products

I first learned about natural skincare when I modelled for the beauty brand LoveLula back in 2010, so I always recommend checking out their website first before going anywhere else. It stocks everything natural in one place, from hair care and body care to nail varnish and make up. It doesn't stock all the products I now use, but it's a great place to start.

I'm starting to trust brands more, and I do trust LoveLula not to put chemical products on their site, because that's what their whole mission statement is. I feel like they do the investigation for me. So I trust them, rather than religiously checking every single ingredient.

It's important to prioritise mental health, so I choose not to worry or obsess about what's in products any more. Everything I do is about not worrying. So if I stay overnight at a friend's and they haven't got natural shampoo and conditioner, I just use what they have. Doing so won't kill me or give me eczema, so I'm a lot more relaxed now.

Product Ingredients I Love

There is nothing more fun than pampering my skin with a mixture of nature in a bottle. Knowing that from head to toe I am being nourished from the outside in. I find it's easier and best for me to just focus on using natural products.

I absolutely LOVE trying new products as long as they are natural. These days, rather than insisting that the products I use have specific ingredients in them, I prefer the products I use avoid having chemicals in them.

I currently use natural moisturising ingredients, such as mango butter, olive leaf oil and shea butter. Other calming anti-inflammatory ingredients include camomile oil and calendula, so look out for those.

I also love anything that includes a rose scent as it's natural and uplifting and girly, and aloe vera, avocado oil and mango butter tend to feature a lot in my products.

Product Ingredients I Avoid:

- parabens;
- synthetic colours;
- phthalates;
- sodium lauryl sulphate;
- sodium benzoate.

(i.e. ALL CHEMICALS, especially the latter two which are drying chemicals). All the above are a bunch of fancy words for chemicals.

If you would like to see the specific products I use, please go to the beauty section on my Youtube channel where I share what works for me.

diy products: how to make your own multi-use product

If I am trying to save money, then I'll just make my own.

To do that I mix 60ml castor oil with 40ml olive oil and a dash of lavender oil. However, it's important to never put essential oil onto broken skin, as that can be dangerous, so I only use that on healed skin. If your skin is not broken, lavender is a good essential oil to use. It will help relax your muscles, it'll help relax your mind. It's also anti-fungal, and an anti-bacterial.

Shake up and use as a deeply nourishing cleanser/moisturiser.

How to use: Apply the oil all over your face and body, leave for 5 minutes and rinse off with a warm flannel. The oils draw out impurities whilst at the same time nourishing the skin, leaving it super moisturised.

I'll put my home-made concoction all over my face and body and then rinse it off in the shower. It's a really thick and gloopy mixture, but it does pull out all the dirt, cleanses your skin, and you don't need to moisturise as well, because your skin is soft already.

When I back-packed across the east coast of Australia with my sister, this came in really handy and never failed me. I packed my home-made product along with a little jar of refreshing rose water and a big tub of aloe vera gel. That's all I needed to travel with for the whole month. No make up, just three natural products, and I felt glowing for the whole adventure.

Since that life-affirming trip I've learned the importance of ensuring that all of the jigsaw pieces fit together.

the whole jigsaw

If I only used moisturisers to manage my eczema, I'd still have it. Skincare is just one part of the puzzle – I also have to work internally as well as externally. I need to consider what I'm eating and putting into my body to avoid any adverse reaction. If I find myself feeling overwhelmed and mentally stressed, or notice I'm thinking in a negative way, that's going to come out via a skin flare-up.

Whenever a flare-up occurs, I now realise it's usually my body's way of notifying me that something isn't quite right and I need to make some adjustments.

Perhaps it's something I've eaten or my environment, and while I can apply a bit of steroid cream to make it go away, that's only a temporary solution. So I need to look at all of the jigsaw pieces, spread them all out across the table and check – what piece do I need to rethink?

- Maybe I need to slow down, maybe I need a bit more sleep?
- Maybe I need to eat a bit more healthily than I have been?
- Perhaps I need to see some friends to help me laugh more and stress less?
- Perhaps I need to put some music on and dance to my favourite tunes?
- Perhaps I need to get into that positive mindset and practice some gratitude statements and affirmations?
- Perhaps I need to move more and book myself into a yoga or workout class?
- Maybe I need to check that I'm on track with my purpose in life?
- Maybe I need a technology detox and a walk in nature?

Each puzzle piece needs to be used to create the picture of health for me. H for Home, O for Optimism, P for Purpose (and Pampering) and E for Eating Well, Exercise and Ecotherapy.

So, about that final part of the puzzle...

"If your body could speak, what would it say?"

DARIA HALPRIN

E is for Eating Well, Exercise and Ecotherapy

the importance of balance

The first thing I was ever any good at was running. That childhood hobby has set me in good stead as an adult. I've been fortunate enough to be sporty and passionate about eating healthily for as long as I can remember.

However, I've also learned the hard way that passion can very easily turn into obsession if there's no balance.

It can be very easy to become obsessive about food and exercise, and obsession with food can lead to all kinds of eating disorders, while obsession with exercise can lead to injury.

Healthy eating and healthy exercise involves balance. Without balance you can find yourself on the extremities of what is healthy.

That's what happened to me. Indeed, the only time I've ever injured myself or veered towards having an eating disorder was when I took things to the extremes, both with food and exercise.

With food, it all came down to avoidance and becoming obsessed with avoiding all the foods on my 'food intolerance' list. So once I discovered that cutting out certain foods might help me reduce my eczema, I became obsessed with avoiding them, and that obsession turned into what is known as orthorexia nervosa, where I became obsessed with eating healthily, rather than not eating at all (anorexia nervosa).

Orthorexia is about being obsessed with 'correct eating', while anorexia means 'without eating'. I ate very little, but what I did eat had to be on my 'good food' list and not on my 'bad food' list. Unfortunately, my 'bad food' list was incredibly long and thus restrictive.

I avoided tomatoes, oranges, even lettuce, which was on my food allergies list. I'd survive either on juice or on a banana for breakfast, a small amount of chicken or fish with vegetables, and then gluten-free cereal for my evening meal. That's obviously not enough food, but back then I saw food as just being enough to fill me for a small amount of time, which decreased my appetite and made me weaker. Ironically, an obsession with being healthy adversely affected my health.

Essentially I was in an avoid zone, rather than a nourish zone. What I put into my body was all focused on 'what can I not eat?', rather than 'what can I eat?'.

Thankfully, having taken my eating to such extremes, I've learned that a healthy balanced diet based on what you CAN eat is the only way to eat in a way that provides your mind and body with enough fuel, whilst also nourishing you with the right balance of nutrients.

With exercise, I also began to take things to the extreme. I used to just run every single morning. Nothing wrong with that, but I wouldn't do anything to relax. So I started replacing the occasional run with a yoga class to achieve a more balanced routine. Now, if my body doesn't feel like running but feels like stretching instead, that's fine. I'll listen to my body now. As long as I exercise four to five times per week, that makes me happy!

Experts suggest we ideally need around 150 minutes of weekly exercise, which amounts to 30 minutes over five days. But those 30 minutes can be broken down into 10 minute slots, such as walking to and from work and doing a 10 minute HIIT routine before lunch.

Eating well and exercising well can become habitual and enjoyable, rather than an obsession.

During my most obsessive period I ran a half-marathon on juice! I had started my work experience for the health company in August, but my eczema was flaring up due to the stress of it all. That September I did the Great North Run, and I ended up injuring myself in the third mile, but I continued to push past the pain, which lead to me not being able to walk properly for weeks afterwards.

That was the beginning of my slide down as I was ill with eczema from then on, went to the Dead Sea at the end of October, and then the following January I was hospitalised. Taking my food and exercise to the extreme without listening to my body (ie my eczema telling me something wasn't right) took its toll.

Since then I've learned the most important word when considering wellbeing is BALANCE. That means a balanced diet, a good balance of aerobic, strength, balance and flexibility exercise and balancing outdoor activity with indoor activity, sitting down with standing up and so on.

The four types of exercise all complement each other and also provide more variety which, for me, makes exercise way more fun. Strength training strengthens muscles which, in turn, helps prevent injury during aerobic exercise as good muscle strength protects and supports our joints. Similarly, balance work improves muscle strength in a way that helps prevent sprains and similar injuries by stabilising movements. Flexibility is also important as it helps avoid muscle pulling and enables better strength training by enabling more joint movement.

e is for exercise: finding your exercise rhythm and routine

> *"Movement is a medicine for creating change in a person's physical, emotional and mental states."*
> **Carol Welch**

The need for a balanced 'diet' of exercise enables you to pick and mix from a range of exercise, from yoga, Pilates or tai chi to walking, running, cycling, swimming, dancing, weight lifting or taking part in team sports like netball or rugby. From tennis, squash and badminton to aerobic workouts, whatever it is, do it because you have decided you like your chosen activity – not because you feel you should. Miserably working out doesn't do your body any favours.

I believe moving your body daily is vital to optimal health, but in a balanced rather than obsessive way. However, unless you enjoy what you're doing, it's difficult to get and stay motivated. I now mix up the four types of exercise into a weekly routine and it's been serving me well over the past few years. I feel toned and energised and, above all, healthy and happy.

In the media we are fed this notion that exercise is only about losing weight and getting our bodies in shape, but it is about so much more than that. As Tony Robbins says, 'motion changes emotion'. Moving your body can truly change the state of how you are feeling.

Exercise reduces inflammation, boosts your mood, improves cardiovascular health, supports your metabolic function and oxygenates your body, which aids digestion too.

For balance and flexibility, I personally LOVE to do Vinyasa yoga (I use the Asana app on my phone), also known as Ashtanga yoga; a fast-paced series of postures or 'asanas' which focuses on flow between movements rather than the actual poses themselves. Hatha yoga focuses on holding each pose through several breaths, so it's worth trying both to see which works best for you and your reasons for doing yoga. I now habitually do a daily yoga practice once or sometimes twice per day, morning and night. This stretches out any tension, provides me with the flexibility and balance types of exercise and helps me refocus my mind to think positively. It also helps me feel in touch with my body and its care.

For my aerobic/cardio exercise I do HIIT (High Intensity Interval Training), and for my strengths training, I lift weights. I also do lots of running and walks in nature whenever I feel like it. So I'm getting a good balance of each of the four main types of exercise.

According to Kelly Drew, an exercise physiologist with the American College of Sports Medicine: "Ideally, you should include all four types of exercise in your workouts. But that doesn't mean you have to do four separate workouts." She suggests combining some exercises together, like strength and balance training. For example, you could do bicep curls while standing on one leg.

Some workouts, such as yoga, incorporate strength, flexibility and balance exercises. But if yoga, Pilates or tai chi aren't your thing, pre- and post-workout stretches to warm up and cool down can provide enough flexibility and balance exercise.

The types of exercise I enjoy I have built up over time, listening and tuning in to what my body enjoys. I find the mixture of them keeps me enthusiastic. In the future, my dream is to learn how to surf. I think that's because of how much I love the sea. Being in the sea brings me back to my true self, which can so often get lost along the journey of life.

There are never-ending ways to move your body, so it's worth testing them out to see which works best for you. I personally enjoy running the most, because it makes me feel free and, with every step, my worries melt away. My regular runs also remind me of my first talent in life, being a good runner!

My advice to anyone starting to build exercise as a habit is to try to find ways to move that you enjoy, as this means you are more likely to exercise more days than not. Aim to do enough to make you sweat, either for 10, 20 or 30 minute intervals.

Moving my body makes me feel like I'm caring for myself and my body, but it's equally important to care about what I put into my body too.

e is for eating well

> *"Let food be thy medicine*
> *and medicine be thy food,"*
> **Hippocrates**

I've made a surprising yet useful discovery during my eczema journey to health, and that is to focus on what you CAN have to eat more than what you CAN'T have. As explained in Chapter 1, when I was allergy tested and given the long list of foods I should no longer eat, I became obsessed with the foods I had to avoid. It took over my life so much that I was no longer in control, my obsession with food took over.

Take tomatoes, for example. When I moved home after university and got together with my boyfriend, he reminded me of the girl I had been before my eczema spiralled out of control. He'd been my best friend since I was 15, and knew me before I'd made any dietary changes. "You used to eat pizza," he reminded me. And when I did eat pizza, I hadn't flared up. He told me he was certain tomatoes wouldn't make me suddenly flare up – but I was convinced they would.

Gradually, somehow, he helped persuade me to start eating normal healthy foods and proper meals again. Not pizza, necessarily, but fish, vegetables and rice and, then, tomato. I had convinced myself I'd end up looking like the person with the swollen head in hospital if I dared to try a tomato, but he said I wouldn't; that if I did he'd come with me to hospital, but that I should at least just try.

Of course, the fear of ever going back to that prevented me from doing so. It wasn't until I started to get stress-induced eczema again and took myself away to London to heal that I found some answers. I'd been having colonics and juicing. Though helpful, it wasn't the answer, and the therapist who refused to massage me (but sat and talked with me instead) suggested yoga in order to realign my body and mind. She also suggested it might be an idea not to avoid so much healthy food – to try to regain that sense of balance.

It felt like a wake-up call to action, so I went back to my hotel room that night and remembered what my boyfriend was saying about tomatoes. And I thought, "I'm going to eat tomatoes now.

I'm going to have a healthy meal and then I'm going to sleep." Right then I decided that that whole week I would get as much sleep as possible and I would eat what normal people eat, except for gluten and dairy. I felt so trapped in my restrictive diet and wanted more freedom with food again.

Eating a healthy balanced diet, spending time with my support network and ramping up the self-care helped me to heal very quickly. Ever since that day I've eaten tomatoes and so much more, and I've not had any kind of food-related flare-up. It just shows how powerful your mind is, because I truly believe that if I had stressed over those tomatoes, I would have flared up.

All those years I spent obsessing about what I needed to avoid, I needn't have done so. At one time I was literally surviving on nuts and juice. All I really needed to do was eat well – and that essentially means eating a healthy balanced diet.

Tomatoes and dairy are in so much, and I'd been using my self-proclaimed allergies to get out of eating anything. So when a friend said, 'I've cooked lasagne', I'd reply, 'Sorry, tomato'. It was a way for me to control what I ate, by using this list of foods to avoid.

Avoidance definitely caused more harm than good as I was deficient in zinc and all kinds of nutrients that our bodies need. It's also worth noting that avoiding foods did not impact my eczema as much as I thought, as I was avoiding foods when I was hospitalised, but I still had the worst eczema of my entire life.

Thankfully, I now know that figuring out a healthy balanced diet based on what you CAN eat, and not what you CAN'T, is the best advice for healthy eating.

There is, for me, a caveat to that. Given that eczema is an inflammatory auto-immune disease, and dairy, gluten and refined sugar are all inflammatory, I recommend avoiding those foods as much as possible. For me, those are three triggers. But, as I've learned since, tomatoes and oranges and all the other foods I avoided are not. Even when you cut those three things out of your diet, there is so much more to try.

Why no gluten? I believe and have experienced it with my own body that foods containing gluten trigger an eczema flare-up. It is a protein found in wheat, rye and barley, and it's been said that the body's immune system can overreact to the gluten protein after it is eaten which can lead to itchy skin and digestive problems. I experienced this and have had to totally cut it out of my diet.

Why no dairy? I myself have had a dramatic improvement with my skin by eliminating dairy from my diet. Again, it seems to be an intolerance that leads to a flare-up. I have read it is one of the most inflammatory foods in our modern diet, and something I highly recommend all eczema sufferers avoid. There are now so many substitute options for dairy products, such as almond, hemp and coconut mylk, and even vegan cheese.

Why no refined sugar? It is highly inflammatory, feeds the bad bacteria in the gut, is highly addictive and full of empty calories, something I like to stay clear of. It also leads to cravings. There are so many options for more natural sweetness in your life, from fresh fruit and berries to the plant stevia, coconut sugar, raw honey and maple syrup.

So once you get those three things out of your body and start feeding yourself with real fresh and beautiful foods, you give yourself the best chance of living an eczema-free life.

The good news is that there are now gluten-free versions of many foods. So I'll have gluten-free porridge for breakfast and replace pasta with rice, quinoa or buckwheat, and I eat lots of vegetables and fish (organic, wherever possible).

I'll also listen to my body. So, if I'm feeling particularly stressed, I'll swap coffee for a matcha tea or hot water with lemon.

Whatever my body is craving I'll make it, whether that's a super-food smoothie, a colourful veggie salad, warm gluten-free oats and a banana or some organic fish and vegetables. These days I keep my diet totally varied and focus on having 'no guilt', no matter what I choose to eat.

That even applies to puddings and sweet food, because there are so many refined sugar-free desserts available to be made.

While I was working with Polly Noble, I learned that chocolate and desserts weren't 'bad food', which is how I had perceived them until that point. I learned you can eat desserts in a healthy way, just by using raw chocolate. Having my 'OMG-I-can-eat-cake-now' moment was a wonderful revelation, as the restriction of having something sweet was lifted and I was now free to eat healthy dessert.

As soon as I discovered the new world of raw food, I began to actually eat food again, rather than just juice, and the world of beautiful whole, natural and organic food choices opened up to me. And what a revelation that has been.

Foods I embrace (whole, natural and organic foods):

- Fresh berries, avocados, lemons, bananas, figs, mangos... the list could go on. I love fruit!
- Fresh colourful vegetables.
- Organic, grass-fed animal protein such as chicken and occasionally beef, though the latter isn't my preference these days.
- All organic fish - my favourites are salmon, shellfish and anchovies.
- Gluten-free grains: quinoa, buckwheat (which are actually seeds and full of protein), gluten-free oats, wholegrain rice.
- Fermented foods such as sauerkraut and kimchi.
- All beans are ok, but I like to soak them first and love to use them for hummus dips.
- Nuts and seeds, activated whenever possible. Pumpkin seeds are full of zinc. Flax and chia seeds are full of omega 3 fatty acids.
- Any dairy-free milks including: almond, hemp, coconut, cashew, rice, and tiger milk.
- Coconut yoghurts
- Sweeteners – raw honey/maple syrup – moderately.
- Oils – olive oil, coconut oil and avocado oil.
- Vinegars – apple cider vinegar.
- Herbs – all.
- Other – raw chocolate (yum!).

Drinks I embrace:

- Spring water
- Hot water with a slice of lemon
- Matcha green tea and herbal teas
- Dairy-free lattes
- Dairy-free hot cacao
- Fresh cold pressed fruit/vegetable juices - Check my food blog for recipes
- Kombucha - A probiotic 'fizzy' drink.

Foods I intuitively don't choose (sugar, dairy, gluten):

- Factory farmed meats, such as hot dogs, pork and cold cuts.
- Processed and fried food
- Gluten-containing grains – wheat, couscous, oats, bran, barley, rye, spelt.
- Dairy-containing food.
- Artificial sweeteners or refined sugars.
- Sunflower oil, canola oil, margarine.
- Commercial salad dressings or sauces.
- Candy and milk chocolate.

Drinks I keep to a minimum (caffeine and alcohol):

- Alcohol – I drink red wine occasionally, when I feel in control of my skin and sometimes gin and tonic or champagne. It all depends on how I feel at the time and the quantity I have. Alcohol is dehydrating and that's not great for anyone's skin. However, I do believe in balance and good company, so don't avoid social occasions as a way to avoid alcohol. Either own who you are and don't have alcohol, or have a small glass or two and drink lemon water inbetween. This book is not about being a skin perfectionist (like I once was), it is about listening to your body. You know more than anyone what is right for you.

- Caffeine-containing energy drinks.
- Commercial fruit juices.

My typical food day totally varies as I always like to mix things up. I currently shop for all my produce on www.ocado.com, but my passion is going to the fresh morning markets abroad to get my food. Ocado is great when you're busy and want everything ordered organic in one place – very convenient for me right now.

Love your gut

I also do what I can to foster a healthy gut. After all, the connection between gut health and mental health has long been established. So much so that our gut is often referred to as our second brain, thanks to the fact that millions of neurons reside in the tissue lining our gastrointestinal tract (our vagus nerve).

These neurons actually communicate with your main brain and, according to a 2017 study into pre-biotics published in the online journal, *Frontiers in Behavioral Neuroscience* by a research team from the University of Colorado, directly impact our stress levels, anxiety, emotions, decision making and even memory. Turns out that this inter-connectedness means the more we look after our gut, and in particular the balance of gut bacteria, the less intrusive stress is likely to be in our lives.

Unbalanced gut bacteria can be caused by prolonged use of steroids and antibiotics, stress itself, low fibre and high sugar diets and regular alcohol consumption.

So how do you maintain a healthy second brain and realign the balance of your gut flora?

1. Eat from the list of foods I embrace above. Lots of vegetables, fermented food, organic food and a reduction in refined sugar and alcohol is seriously beneficial to gut health.
2. Drink more water. In fact, drink mostly water. Make water your main drink which you sip regularly. You could even set an alarm to remind you to drink water on the hour every hour to keep you hydrated.
3. Consume both probiotics and prebiotics. Probiotics introduce good bacteria to your gut, while prebiotics feed the bacteria which already exists. According to research, prebiotics protect gut microbes from stress-induced disruptions and can also help with the recovery of normal sleep patterns which can be adversely affected by stress.

A little extra help

The following supplements have helped me:

1. One probiotic every morning to replenish the 'good bacteria' in my gut and give my body the best possible health defence. Getting the right supplements is key, and I only trust certain brands.

2. A digestive enzyme with every meal, when I remember. This supports my body in breaking down my food and therefore in absorbing vital nutrients. We naturally have digestive enzymes in our salivary glands and small intestines, but I have found these digestive enzymes to be very beneficial in the early stages of healing my skin.

3. Zinc. I usually take this with my lunch. Zinc is such an important mineral, and five years ago I was 20% deficient so I like to keep this in check. Zinc isn't found in many plant-based foods and I only eat meat minimally, so this supplement gives me a balance of zinc.

4. Magnesium. Before bed I enjoy drinking a magnesium supplement. I have found the powder works much better than any tablet and is a tasty evening drink. I love the Natural Calm brand.

5. I sometimes take a 'Triphala Plus' supplement in the evening by the Pukka brand. I have found it to be beneficial in maintaining regularity, which is an absolute must for keeping your body clean and skin glowing. It naturally assists in internal cleansing, supports digestion and absorption, rejuvenates tissues and is a natural antioxidant. For anyone in the early stages of cleansing, I find this supplement extremely beneficial in reducing any 'detox symptoms' that may arise.

6. Finally, milk thistle – this flower herb has been a life saver for me over the years. It helps detoxify the liver and since Louise Hay says anger is held in the liver, I believe it helps me get though stressful times in my life, helps me bounce back from flare-ups better and, if I do decide to drink alcohol, it really supports my skin.

e is for ecotherapy

"Look deep into nature, and then you will understand everything better."
Albert Einstein

I always knew it felt *good* to be outdoors in nature, but I didn't realise the science behind it until recently. I didn't know what ecotherapy was, let alone how it worked. All I knew was how the sea powerfully brought me back to me; to my ultimate happy zone.

Of course, we've long known that eating well and moving our bodies is important, but it has been less well-known that where you go to move your body is equally relevant to your wellbeing. In recent years, the power of nature as a nourisher has been making the health headlines.

Being outdoors in the fresh air, amongst nature, can do wonders for wellbeing levels. In fact, it's now been proven that spending time outside, in nature, makes us healthier and happier.

Nowadays, if I ever feel out of whack, I'll check to see if I've been out in nature that day, whether I've done any exercise and what I've been putting into my body. Luckily I've cultivated some good healthy habits around exercise and eating, but now I also take myself on daily walks in nature, which is especially helpful when I feel I've spent too much time on technology and need to get out of my head.

Nature connects me to my true self and offers a revitalising energy. The fresh air, the beautiful scenery, it has such a positive effect that I've now made it a non-negotiable part of my daily life and always ensure I schedule some ecotherapy into my lunch-time breaks.

Being in nature helps me clear my mind and feel truly alive. Whether it's walking among pine and yew trees in local woodland, running through a local park or, my favourite, bathing in the sea, nature nurtures and nourishes me.

Finnish researchers who've measured wellbeing and levels of stress and anxiety before and after 20 minute walks have discovered, and reported in *The Journal of Environmental Psychology*, there is a remarkable difference between those who have walked in urban settings or through shopping centres, and those who've walked in green spaces. Only the latter have seen a huge boost in their wellbeing levels and a significant reduction in their stress levels.

Nature has incredible healing qualities, so much so that ecotherapy is now being prescribed for stress and anxiety. This is because natural landscapes stimulate our 'rest and digest' parasympathetic nervous system and soothe our 'fight or flight' sympathetic nervous system.

But what exactly is ecotherapy?

Well, ecotherapy refers to any outdoor activity which positively impacts our mental and physical wellbeing. From gardening and the pleasure of tending to plants and watching them grow to forest-bathing, green exercise (such as cycling or horse-riding) or outdoor conservation work, there's a wide range of activities to choose from.

Forest bathing simply means mindfully walking and breathing in woodland where there is a dense setting of trees and plants.

In Japan, Shinrin-yoku (otherwise known as 'forest bathing') has been part of a public health programme for over 30 years. This is because the essential oils emitted by trees have now been proven to help boost our immune system while reducing the production of stress hormone cortisol.

Our immune system protects us from infection by destroying any viruses or bacteria or parasites which it doesn't recognise. Trees and plants emit essential oils called phytoncides to protect themselves, and it is these which can help improve the functionality of our own immune system as we breathe in fresh forest air. These protective and healing qualities are of particular note to eczema sufferers, for obvious reasons. We need all the help we can get with our immune system functionality.

How wonderful it is that simply being outside in nature can be such a powerful way to protect ourselves? No wonder I always feel better and less stressed after bathing in the salty sea, or after I've been for a walk or run through woodland or across green landscapes.

Swedish studies have also discovered that outdoor walks can help us to think more clearly, which is why I always head outside for a stroll before important meetings or working on creative projects.

Even having a view of trees from indoors can boost wellbeing, as studies in the 1980s showed that hospital patients who looked out onto natural landscapes healed quicker than those who looked out onto a view of a car park or brick wall. Even indoor gardening for patients unable to venture outdoors has been proven to have positive effects on mental health.

Switching off and reconnecting with nature, replacing screen time with green time and just putting down our phones to take a break outside has been shown to give our bodies and minds a chance to reset. That's why ecotherapy is such an important part of my own HOPE Principles and self-care recipe.

Whether I venture out into the woods, mindfully pay attention to what's around me in outdoor landscapes by focusing on what I can see, hear and feel, or schedule a visit to the seaside or plan outdoor adventures, regular outdoor time is a must in my book.

Here is something which is absolutely free, yet gives us so much to boost our physical and mental health, both of which are vital to how much or how little eczema we endure. And what a beautiful way to spend time – outdoors in nature.

It certainly makes sense to include ecotherapy in my HOPE Principles, because everything I do has a natural theme and is about finding that NATURAL balance: being in NATURE, using NATURAL skincare, eating organic NATURAL foods and spending time with people in environments I NATURALLY feel aligned with and supported by.

So here's to nature, and it guiding us back to a more natural way of living.

CHAPTER 11

My Recipes, Cafés, Retreats and Books

What you eat, where you eat and where you go to get your skin, mind, body and soul rejuvenated and replenished is important. The good news is, wellness is a hot topic at the moment, so a multitude of cafés focusing on natural organic food have sprung up across the globe. Here I'll share some of my favourites, along with some of my top travel tips and how to create your own retreat wherever you are.

As a natural food chef, I've included recipes too.

The directory also includes a list of books that I've used in combination to boost my spirits and be in control of my skin.

my favourite wellness cafés worldwide

England

- The Garden Hale, Manchester.
- Elvens Café, Manchester.
- Earthlings Inn, Bolton.
- Palm Vaults, Shoreditch, London.
- Farm Girl Café, Notting Hill, London.
- The Grind, Shoreditch, London.
- Redemption, Shoreditch, London.
- Tanya's Raw Café, London.
- The Attendant Café, Shoreditch, London.
- Farmacy Café, Notting Hill, London.

Australia

- Combi, Elwood, Melbourne.
- The Grounds, Alexandria, Sydney.
- Acai Brothers, Bondi Beach, Sydney.

Canada

- Flurples, Sudbury, ON (Vegan ice cream).
- Beards, Sudbury, ON (Vegan coffee and bakery).
- Tucos Taco Lounge, Sudbury, ON (Vegan Mexican).
- The Laughing Bydda, Sudbury, ON (Gluten-free, dairy-free pizza)!
- Salute Coffee, Sudbury, ON (Dairy-free coffee with pure maple syrup).

France

- Bio Market, Port Grimard, Saint Tropez.
- Acai Spot, Saint Tropez.
- Café Pinson, Paris.
- Bol Porridge, Paris.
- Hardware Society, Paris.
- Cojean, Paris.
- Wild and the Moon, Paris.

Malta

- Dr Juice, St Julians (plus five other locations across the island).
- Emma's Kitchen, San Gwann (The best chocolate truffles).

Netherlands

- Blushing, Amsterdam.
- Roots, Amsterdam.

Spain

- Flax & Kale Café, Barcelona.
- Teresa's Juicery, Barcelona.
- Passion Café, Ibiza.
- Montressol Hotel, Ibiza.
- Bali Bowls, Ibiza.
- Atzaro Spa, Ibiza.
- Cocos Deli, Palma.
- Real Food Camp, Malaga. (Great for kids and educating them on how to cook healthy food).

USA

- The Ale House, Venice, LA.
- The Hive, Santa Monica, LA.
- Gratitude Café, Venice, LA.
- Ground Work Coffee, Venice, LA.
- Malibu Farm Café, Malibu, LA.
- Urth Café, Laguna, LA.
- Eat By Chloe, New York.

retreats

In my mind, I had been to so many retreats I'd have plenty to list in this directory section of the book. However, when I sat down to write them all out, I realised – I've actually always created my own retreats based on wherever I am staying.

I am incredibly lucky that I get to stay at my family home in the south of France.

Whenever I am there I:

- immerse myself in nature;
- go on daily runs by the sea;
- exercise in the outdoor gym;
- eat from the fresh fruit in our garden;
- make juices and prepare healthy food for the family.

It always felt like I was running a mini retreat whenever we'd have guests stay throughout summer. Now, when I go on holiday, I do the same: I create ideal retreats for myself wherever I am.

I've only been on a few actual retreats myself, one in Israel (the Dead Sea experience), another yoga retreat in Wales and I worked as a chef in Tuscany for a fitness retreat.

So, instead of pretending I have been to all of the best retreats in the world, I thought I'd share with you how I create my own retreats, wherever I am in the world, so you can do the same.

How To Feel Like You're On A Retreat, Even When You're Not

I feel I am a pro at this. It is basically investing TLC into yourself wherever you are. For me, I like to pick a peaceful sunshine location where I can focus on solitude and healing. If you can't chase the sunshine, then get out into nature. If it's raining, wear a raincoat and brave it, because this retreat feeling is possible to achieve anywhere!

This is what a typical day on my own inner retreat would look like:

- **Sleep**: Wake up around 8-9am with no structure, just to feel well rested and caught up on sleep. Sleep is so healing for your skin.
- **Hydrate and move**: Next I'd hydrate with lots of lemon water and get my body moving. This could be through yoga or a run surrounded by nature, ideally the sea.
- **Pamper and nourish**: I'd then cleanse and pamper myself in natural products and make a nourishing plant-based breakfast.
- **Set a positive mindset**: After breakfast, I would write my positive intentions for the day, and say my affirmations in the mirror.
- **Adventure time**: Then, I'd go off exploring. I would try and find new hike trails or go off exploring a town I have never ventured to before. This could be alone or with another adventure buddy. The world is such an incredibly inspiring place with so much beauty around every corner. It's no secret I have a Wanderlust, but even in England I would rather road trip to new areas than sit still in a routine.

Adventures always fill up my soul. I would take a book in my bag, just in case I wanted a break on the beach or at a café to read something uplifting.

- **Cook and have company**: In the afternoon I would probably spend it cooking up new recipes or get ready for an evening meal with good company. Any activity that gets me out and about or around new people. Even if it is a Skype call with one of my international friends, this ALWAYS lifts my spirits.

- **Bathe and meditate**: My night would then end in smiles, laughter and perhaps a salt bath, meditation and a good night's sleep.

I have this self-care checklist when I need to feel my soul. I wanted to share it as a source of inspiration to fill yours up too. Feel free to add to the list.

- Say affirmations.
- Update my vision board.
- Write in my gratitude journal.
- Pamper with beauty products or go for a treatment.
- Listen to positive music.
- Read an uplifting book or quote of the day (see Books section).
- Sweat it out – gym, run, walk or just sit in a sauna!
- Drink more water – cleanse and hydrate.
- Eat like you love yourself – intuitive eating.
- Listen to your inner child and write in a notebook what she/he really needs.
- Call a good friend.
- Make a list of everything you are proud of yourself for.

my top skincare travel tips

1. Move your body before and after flying. A yoga flow is perfect to stretch out the kinks and get the blood flowing before or after you've been sitting still for ages.

2. Eat before your flight or prep your own food box for a long-haul journey, as you can't be sure the food on the plane will be best for your eczema.

3. Stay hydrated. This is so important! Sometimes, I even add extra electrolyte drops to my water bottle.

4. Stay calm and positive. Listen to a guided meditation or to positive music. Write in your gratitude journal.

5. Make a self-care package. I take lavender oil, a crystal, colloidal silver, a mini cleanser and moisturiser and hydration eye gels so I can pamper on the go.

6. Read an uplifting book.

7. Take travel probiotics! Remember, healthy gut = healthy mind = healthy skin.

8. Take a sleep mask and have a little snooze en route to your destination.

recipes

Here I share with you five days of nutritious and delicious recipes. Since this book isn't a 'cook book', I have kept all the recipes reasonably simple for you and you can watch how I make them on YouTube. Please feel free to be creative and tweak them as you desire.

I found that avoiding gluten, dairy and refined sugars really helped my skin, so you won't find any of those in these recipes. I believe in intuitive eating and not labelling myself. As you read earlier, it is really important for me not to make 'rules' around what food I can't eat for the sake of my mental health and zinc deficiency concerns. Therefore, these recipes are mainly plant-based but contain the odd piece of fish or optional meat.

I am not saying what I eat is 'right' for everyone, or that it will heal your eczema, and you don't have to stick to this plan. I'm simply sharing these recipes to give you some food inspiration. I eat organic, grass-fed and locally sourced whenever possible.

For more recipe ideas please visit thebeautyofeczema.com.

Day 1 - Breakfast: Chocolate/Vanilla Protein Porridge

Ingredients:

- 40g gluten-free oats (I like the sprouted version, but it isn't necessary)
- 1 cup of water or almond milk
- 1 scoop vegan protein
- 1 tbsp almond butter
- handful of berries or goji berries, or 1 banana

Instructions:

1. Warm the oats and milk/water in a saucepan for a couple of minutes.
2. Stir in the protein powder.
3. Top with the nut butter and fruit of choice.

Super tasty and totally gluten- and dairy free.

Lunch: Oh Mega Salmon

Ingredients:

- 1 salmon fillet (around 100g)
- 100g asparagus
- 100g sweet potatoes, chopped into cubes
- a dash of almond milk
- a dash of maple syrup
- 10g olive oil (or coconut oil or avocado oil)
- 20g chopped onion (brunoise style)
- 30g chopped tomatoes (large brunoise style)

Instructions:

1. Steam the salmon over a pan simmering with water until cooked all the way through.
2. Steam or boil the broccoli in another pan, and the same with the sweet potatoes.
3. When the sweet potatoes are soft, drain the water from the pan then add a dash of almond milk and maple syrup, and mash them until they go creamy.
4. Pour 10g of your oil preference into a saucepan and cook the chopped onion and tomatoes. Keep the heat low to avoid burning the oil.
5. Place everything on your plate, sprinkle with black pepper and salt, and enjoy!

Dinner: Colourful Quinoa Bowl

Ingredients:

- 100g quinoa
- 50g fresh peppers, chopped brunoise style
- 1 handful of parsley, finely chopped
- ¼ red onion, small dice
- 1 tbsp olive oil
- 1 tbsp cider vinegar
- pinch of salt
- 1 tablespoon of pumpkin seeds
- additional extra: chicken/ salmon/seabass fillet

Instructions:

1. Boil the quinoa for 15 minutes until soft and fluffy.
2. Drain the water from the quinoa, then add to a bowl, throw in the parsley, onion, peppers and pumpkin seeds and toss together.
3. Drizzle with olive oil, cider vinegar, salt and pumpkin seeds.

Day 2 - Breakfast: Overnight Chia Pudding

Ingredients:

- 1 cup of almond milk
- 3 tbsp chia seeds
- 1 small handful of berries
- 1 tsp maple syrup or honey if desired
- Additional extra: a tablespoon of cacao powder to make it chocolate flavoured.

Instructions:

1. Mix all ingredients in a small bowl, leave overnight and enjoy in the morning.

Lunch: Baked Sweet Potato & Home-made Avocado Pesto

Ingredients:

- 1 sweet potato
- avocado pesto dressing: 1 handful of basil leaves, 1 tbsp pine nuts, 1 tbsp olive oil, 1 tbsp of cider vinegar, ½ avocado
- 1 handful of mixed salad leaves
- 1/4 cucumber, diced
- additional extra: 1 chicken fillet

Instructions:

1. Bake the sweet potato in the oven for 45 mins–1 hour, until soft and tender.
2. Chop the chicken into cubes and cook in olive oil or coconut oil or avocado oil (Whichever your personal preference is; make sure not to over heat the oil).
3. Blend the ingredients of the avocado pesto dressing in a Nutribullet.
4. Plate up the salad with cucumber on top, place the sweet potato and chicken on top and drizzle with the avocado pesto. Enjoy!

Dinner: Seabass, Cauliflower & Rice/Buckwheat Noodles

Ingredients:

- 100g seabass fillet
- 100g rice/buckwheat noodles
- 100g cauliflower, (chopped into bite-sized florets)
- dash of tamari sauce (gluten-free)
- pinch of salt and pepper

Instructions:

1. Steam/poach the seabass fillet in a frying pan with boiling water.
2. Boil the cauliflower.
3. Boil the rice/buckwheat noodles.
4. Plate up with the noodles first, cauliflower on top, then the seabass.
5. Drizzle with Tamari sauce, Himilayan salt and pepper.

Day 3 - Breakfast: Avocado Toast

Ingredients:

- 1 slice of gluten-free bread or grain-free bread (recipe in Snacks)
- ½ avocado
- pinch of salt & pepper
- 1 tsp cider vinegar
- 3 chopped baby tomatoes
- 1 tsp olive oil
- additional extra: chilli flakes

Instructions:

1. Place the bread in the toaster or grill in the oven.
2. Mash the avocado with olive oil, cider vinegar, salt and pepper.
3. Spread onto the toast, place the tomatoes on top and sprinkle with chilli flakes.
4. You can double the recipe up if this is too small a portion for you.

Lunch: Broccoli 'Gut Healing' Soup

Ingredients:

- ½ tbsp oil (either olive oil, coconut oil or avocado oil)
- ¼ onion, diced
- 1 garlic clove, peeled and chopped
- 100g broccoli
- ½ potato, peeled and chopped
- 200ml gluten-free stock
- pinch of nutmeg, salt and pepper
- additional extra: chicken bone broth – great for healing the gut

(To make chicken bone broth, boil a chicken carcass in a slow cooker for 6-12 hours– I usually leave it overnight. You then strain the chicken bones and pop the liquid in the fridge. It will set into a jelly mixture, with sometimes a butter-like topping. Scrape this off, as it is the fat, and add the jelly mixture to any soups for gut-healing benefits.)

Instructions:

1. Heat your chosen oil in a saucepan and sweat the onions and garlic until soft.
2. Add the stock, nutmeg, salt, pepper, broccoli and potatoes and boil for around 15 minutes.
3. Pour in a blender until smooth or chunky, as desired.
4. Pour into a bowl and enjoy!

Dinner: Grass-fed Fillet Steak with a Red Wine Sauce / Vegan Burger with Veggies

Ingredients:

- 1 x fillet steak – omit if vegan/vegetarian and add quinoa, buckwheat or vegan burger from Amy's Kitchen (Amys.com)
- 1 tsp coconut oil
- 100g spinach, steamed
- 50g asparagus
- 100g parsnip
- dash of almond milk
- dash of red wine
- 1 tsp maple syrup

Note: I very, very rarely eat red meat (but sometimes need to due to my zinc deficiency – see page 21). When I do it is always the highest quality, locally sourced, organic and grass-fed.

Instructions:

1. In a saucepan, steam the spinach and asparagus and set aside.
2. Boil the parsnip until soft, drain the water from the parsnip then add a tsp of maple syrup, dash of almond milk and pinch of salt, and mash until creamy.
3. In a small frying pan on low heat, using the oil of your choice, cook the steak for as long as desired to your taste. (I enjoy it medium-rare so I cook both sides for a couple of minutes).
4. Add the red wine and let the steak absorb this in the warm pan.
5. Plate everything up and enjoy!

Day 4 - Breakfast: Banana & Spiced Nut Butter on Toast

Ingredients:

- 1 slice of gluten-free bread or grain-free bread (recipe in Snacks)
- 1 tbsp nut butter (store-bought, or check the Snacks section for recipes)
- On Guard doTERRA oil, or cinnamon powder
- 1 x banana, chopped

Instructions:

1. Pop the bread in the toaster or grill in the oven for a couple of minutes.
2. Spread the nut butter on the toast and add 1 drop of the oil or a pinch of cinnamon.
3. Place the banana on top and enjoy.

Lunch: Smoked Salmon Courgetti

Ingredients:

- 100g courgette
- 50g carrot
- 5 sprigs of chives
- 5 olives, chopped
- 5 sundried tomatoes, chopped
- 100g smoked salmon
- 1 tbsp olive oil
- 1 tablespoon lemon juice
- pinch of salt and pepper

Instructions:

1. Spiralise the courgette and carrot and pop in a bowl.
2. Finely chop the chives and add to the bowl along with the olives and sundried tomatoes.
3. Chop the smoked salmon into small pieces and add to the bowl with the olive oil, lemon juice, salt and pepper.
4. Mix together, and enjoy.

Dinner: Vegan Nachos

Ingredients:

- 1 x bag gluten-free nachos
- 1 x sweet potato
- ½ cup boiling water
- 1 cup soaked cashews
- 4 tbsp nutritional yeast
- 1 tbsp cider vinegar
- 1 red pepper, finely diced
- 2 chopped gherkins
- chopped jalapenos (handful)
- pinch of cayenne pepper
- additional extra: black beans, or diced chicken

Instructions:

1. Pour the gluten-free nachos into a bowl.
2. Make the vegan cheese by boiling the sweet potato until soft, and popping into a blender along with the boiling water (you may need to add more depending on the size of the potato), soaked cashews, nutritional yeast and cider vinegar.
3. Pour the cheese over the nachos.
4. Sprinkle over with chopped peppers, gherkins, jalapenos and add a pinch of cayenne pepper.
5. Enjoy!

Day 5 - Breakfast: Strawberry Smoothie Bowl

Ingredients:

- 100g frozen strawberries
- 1 banana
- 1 scoop of protein
- 1 cup of almond milk
- additional extras: 1tsp maca powder, 1tsp chia seeds, raw blueberry powder
- Topping options: fresh berries, hemp seeds, coconut flakes, raw honey, bee pollen, gluten-free granola, cacao nibs.

Instructions:

1. Blend the strawberries, banana, protein, almond milk and additional extras.
2. Pour into a bowl and top with whatever toppings you desire. The above are my favourites.

Lunch: Beauty Burrito

Ingredients:

- 1 gluten-free wrap
- 1 chicken fillet, diced (optional)
- ¼ avocado, mashed
- handful of chopped parsley
- ½ small red onion, diced
- ½ tomato, diced
- ¼ can of black beans
- additional extras: chopped gherkins, garlic powder, olive oil, cider vinegar, vegan mayo

Instructions:

1. Steam your chicken, or cook on a low heat in either: coconut oil, olive oil or avocado oil.
2. Warm the black beans in a pan and blend into a paste.
3. Pop the bean paste onto the wrap, top with the avocado, parsley, onion and tomato, add the chicken and any additional extras.
4. Wrap up and enjoy!

Dinner: Seaweed Pasta

Ingredients:

- 50g cooked brown rice noodles
- 50g seaweed spaghetti (I use the brand Atlantic Kitchen) or kelp noodles
- 30g mushrooms
- 30g red onions
- tamari sauce or hemp pesto from the brand Pro Fusion

Instructions:

1. Boil the rice noodles and seaweed in a pan for 10 minutes.
2. Cook the mushrooms and onions on a low heat in either: coconut oil, avocado oil or olive oil until soft.
3. Drain the water from the noodles and seaweed.
4. Mix the noodles, seaweed, mushrooms and onions together in a bowl.
5. Drizzle with tamari or hemp pesto. (I recommend Pro Fusion hemp pesto).
6. Enjoy!

Drinks

- Celery juice – 1 bunch of celery, juiced. I love to drink this most mornings now, thanks to the Medical Medium! For more juice and smoothie recipes, please keep an eye out on my food blog here : www.thebeautyofeczema.com
- Lemon water – ¼ lemon squeezed into water.
- Hot cacao – 1 teaspoon of cacao powder with 1 cup of warm almond milk and a tsp of maple syrup, and a dash of On Guard essential oil by doTERRA.
- Turmeric latte – 1 teaspoon of turmeric, ½ teaspoon of ginger, ½ teaspoon of cinnamon, a pinch of black pepper, 1 cup of coconut milk and 1 teaspoon of honey.
- Kombucha

Snacks and Desserts

- Raw chocolate.
- A handful of fresh berries, blueberries are my favourite!
- A handful of olives.

Dates with Nut Butter

Ingredients:

- 5 Medjool dates
- 5 teaspoons of nut butter

Instructions:

1. Slice open each Medjool date and remove the stone.
2. Scoop 1 teaspoon of chosen nut butter into each date.
3. Enjoy!

Nut Butter Recipes

Spiced Chocolate Hazelnut:

- 300g of hazelnuts
- 3 tbsp maple syrup
- dash of On Guard oil
- pinch of salt

Honey & Vanilla Cashew Butter:

- 250g cashews
- 1 tsp vanilla powder
- 1 tsp honey
- pinch of salt

Salted Peanut Butter:

- 500g peanuts
- 1 tsp salt

Instructions for all (see my YouTube video for more details):

- Add ingredients to a food processor.
- Blend for around 10 minutes until smooth and creamy.

Raw Berry Cheesecake (See My YouTube Channel)

Ingredients (base):

- 150g cashews (soaked for 6 hours or overnight)
- 100g walnuts (soaked for 6 hours or overnight)
- ¼ tsp Himalayan salt
- 2 tbsp maple syrup
- 2 tbsp coconut oil

Ingredients (filling):

- 320g cashew nuts (soaked overnight)
- 3 tbsp maple syrup
- 185g frozen raspberries
- 65g frozen cherries
- 60g coconut oil (melted)
- desiccated coconut, extra raspberries/cherries and edible flowers (if in season) for decoration

Instructions:

1. Soak all of your nuts – ideally the day before or, if you have forgotten, pop them in some hot water as a last resort.
2. Weigh out all the ingredients.
3. Add all the 'base ingredients' to a food processor. Grind until everything starts sticking together. You don't want this base to be super smooth, chunky is great.
4. Line a cake tin with clingfilm – this makes it easier to pull the cheesecake out once ready.
5. Pour the base into the cake tin, and press down firmly with your hands until it covers the entire base.

6. Pop into the freezer to harden.

7. Rinse the food processor and begin to make the filling.

8. Pour the cashew nuts into the food processor and blend until super smooth and creamy.

9. Add the rest of the ingredients and again process until smooth.

10. Pull out the base from the freezer and pour the raspberry filling on top. It should be a beautiful bright pink colour.

11. I would then decorate it with extra frozen raspberries and cherries and a sprinkle of desiccated coconut.

12. Pop the cake tin back into the freezer to continue setting for the next 3 hours, until completely firm.

13. Take out of the freezer and chop into slices, ready to be enjoyed.

14. If you would prefer to watch a video on how to make this, follow the link to my YouTube channel where you can follow along and we can make it together.

Vegan Protein Banana Ice Cream

Ingredients:

- 1 frozen banana
- 2 dashes of almond mylk
- ½ scoop of vegan vanilla protein

Instructions:

1. Blend everything in a Nutribullet until smooth.
2. Pour into a bowl and enjoy.

Bounty Bars (See My YouTube Channel)

Ingredients (base):

- 250g desiccated coconut
- ⅔cup coconut oil
- ⅓ cup maple syrup
- 1 tsp vanilla powder
- 2 tbsp beetroot powder

Ingredients (top layer):

- ⅔ cup coconut oil
- 100g maple syrup
- ½ tsp vanilla powder
- 3 tbsp cacao powder
- rose petals for decoration

Instructions:

1. Add all base ingredients to a food processor and blend until fully combined.
2. Add the mixture to an 8 x 10 inch cake tin.
3. Pop in the freezer whilst you make the top layer.
4. Whizz all the top layer ingredients together in a Nutribullet.
5. Remove the base from the freezer and pour this chocolate mixture on top.
6. Pop back into the freezer for 2 hours.
7. After 2 hours, remove, chop into bite-size pieces and enjoy!

Beetroot Hummus with Crudities (See My YouTube Channel)

Ingredients:

- 240g chickpeas
- 100g cooked beetroot
- juice of 1 lemon
- 5 tbsp olive oil
- 2 garlic cloves
- 1 tsp Himalayan salt
- 2 tbsp tahini
- sesame seeds to decorate
- for crudities – 1 carrot, 1 celery stick, ¼ cucumber

Instructions:

1. Add all the ingredients into a food processor and blend until smooth.
2. Chop vegetables into chunky wedges for dipping.

Seeded Crackers/Flat Bread

This is perfect with the beetroot hummus.

Ingredients:

- 90g pumpkin seeds
- 40g sunflower seeds
- 50g of quinoa flakes
- 1 tbsp nutritional yeast flakes
- 100g gluten-free teff flour
- 1 tsp sea salt
- 100ml olive oil
- 120ml water
- spices or herbs

Instructions:

1. Pre-heat the oven to 175 degrees.
2. Measure out the dry ingredients and combine together in a mixing bowl.
3. Add the olive oil to the dry ingredients and stir.
4. Add the water and set aside for 7 minutes until it looks a little like porridge.
5. Put the dough on baking parchment on a baking tray.
6. Place another sheet of baking paper on top, and roll the dough out.
7. Gently remove the top sheet of baking paper, and place tray in the oven.
8. Bake for 15-20 minutes until brown.
9. Take out and leave to cool, then using your hands break up into 'cracker size' pieces.

Grain-Free Bread

Ingredients:

- 150g buckwheat flour
- 100g arrowroot
- ½ tsp Himalayan salt
- ½ tsp bicarbonate of soda
- 4 tbsp nutritional yeast
- 5-6 eggs – or vegan eggs using flaxseed/chia seeds, see below
- 1 tsp apple cider vinegar
- 2 tbsp chives, finely chopped
- 50g pitted olives
- 2-3tbsp pumpkin seeds
- 2 tbsp coconut oil

(To make a vegan flax egg, mix 2½ teaspoons of flaxseeds with water until it forms a jelly substance. To make a chia egg, combine 1 tbsp chia seeds with 2½tbsp water.)

Instructions:

1. Pre-heat the oven to 160 degrees and wipe a loaf tin with the coconut oil to prevent the mixture sticking to the tin.
2. Mix all your dry ingredients together in a bowl – the buckwheat flour, arrowroot, Himalayan salt, nutritional yeast and bicarbonate of soda.
3. In another bowl mix the other ingredients – the eggs, cider vinegar, chives and olives.
4. Combine the ingredients from both bowls until it forms a doughy consistency.

5. Pour the mixture into the loaf tin prepared earlier and sprinkle your pumpkin seeds on top. Then place it in the oven for 30 minutes. Keep an eye on it as it may need more or less time, depending on your oven.

6. When ready, remove from the oven to cool for 5 minutes.

7. Chop into slices and enjoy for the next 3 days.

Note: I like to top mine with olive tapenade, coconut oil or hummus. Experiment and see how you like to enjoy yours.

Ready Prepared Foods

What about convenience foods, when you just don't have the time to cook from scratch?

Amy's Kitchen frozen foods are my go-to when I need a quick meal and I don't have time to cook. (We are all human)!

They can be purchased on www.ocado.co.uk along with gluten-free cereals, dairy-free mylks, nut butters – everything you need to live a gluten-free, dairy-free and sugar-free lifestyle.

some book suggestions you may enjoy

- Mel Wells – *The Goddess Revolution* and *Hungry For More*
- Louise Hay – *You Can Heal Your Life*
- Chloe Brotheridge – *The Anxiety Solution*
- Rhonda Byrne – *The Secret*
- Paulo Coelho – *The Alchemist*
- Persia Lawson and Joey Bradford – *The Inner Fix*
- Heather Askinosie and Timmi Jandro – *Crystal Muse*
- Daniel Chidiac – *Who Says You Can't? You Do*
- Cheryl Rickman – *The Flourish Handbook*

"There were moments when it hurt so bad you couldn't breathe, yet somehow you survived the pain. There were days when you could barely put one foot in front of the other, yet somehow you arrived at your destination. There were nights when you cried yourself to sleep, yet somehow you held on until the morning. Your life is nothing less than a miracle."

E L E A N O R   B R O W N N

Conclusion

So, lovely, you've made it this far, but your journey has just begun.

My wish for you is that you now feel supported, like you are not alone and are full of HOPE, ready to live a life beyond eczema.

Can you see the beauty in it now? I hope so!

Let it guide you, let it teach you, and watch your life transform.

I have learnt over time that the more I tried to 'control' my skin condition, the angrier it got. Trust me when I say, your skin doesn't want to be controlled; it wants to be listened to, understood and loved.

As you've read, my eczema has led me towards finding and developing the HOPE Principles, which I would not have discovered had I not had eczema. Not only that, in using what I've learned on my journey to help people like you, I am able to attribute significant meaning to my entire journey – the ups and the downs, the rough and the smooth. I believe we can all see the beauty in eczema if we choose to do so.

If you can find meaning in what you have gone through, or are still going through, I believe, that is the start of truly owning who you are, ready for a stronger and more positive future. If you see eczema as a beautiful part of your journey, which has helped you learn to listen to your body, which has helped you seek out solutions and, in doing so find this book and realise just how powerful your mind is, then you have found the magic puzzle piece.

And if you pass this book on to someone else who is suffering from the world's most common skin condition, you can give even more meaning to what you've gone through too.

I'm so grateful for all I've been through, because it's part of the bigger picture of my life and it's made me who I am. And I'm grateful that I discovered the bigger picture jigsaw of health, and all the jigsaw pieces that fix together to create it, because now I am free to thrive in my life and to empower others to do the same.

Thank you for reading this book. I hope you find my story and the tools explored within it not only helpful, but supportive, like a warm hug from someone who truly understands the journey you are on.

May you be eczema-free for as long as possible; and, even more importantly, may you feel able to view your eczema journey as beautifully guiding and empowering. For we are the sum of all our experiences, good and bad, and we become stronger as we navigate our way through them. Navigating our way through difficult times further demonstrates hope, and hope is sometimes all we need to get us through whatever obstacles stand in our way.

You've got this, and I have got your back!

Lots of love and positive vibes,

Acknowledgements

Thank you to everyone who has been part of this journey - your presence made such an impact on the woman I am today.

Thank you Louise Hay. If it wasn't for you, I never would have realised the strong correlation between my mind and body. The book '*You Can Heal Your Life*' was a catalyst for my healing journey.

Thank you Cheryl. From the moment we met, I knew you were the woman to help me create this book. You have supported me from beginning to end in getting this book out in the world and for that I am so deeply grateful.

Thank you to the incredible women behind the scenes, Shannon, Louise and, in particular, Carol and Summer, I deeply appreciate your time and support in getting this book out into the world, and for believing in me and my mission. You are the true rocks behind what I do.

Thank you Dad, for your consistent love, friendship and support with this journey I am on. Thank you for backing this book 100% and for your unwavering belief in me. You taught me hard times don't last forever; to never give up and that a strong mind can overcome anything. You were right. I love you.

Thank you Mum, for your unconditional love, wisdom, and forever caring vibes. You guided me to all the breakthroughs and were by my side in hospital up until the day I healed. You believed I would get through my darkest days and that belief kept me going each day. Your strong mind and soft heart inspires me. I love you.

Thank you to my best friends, my small yet international circle I am so blessed to have in my life. You helped me 'own my skin condition', taught me that it didn't define me and helped me learn to love myself. The countless messages, voice notes and 'Facetimes' during the stressful times while I've been writing this book have meant so much. You have been there when I needed you the most; you refused to let me give up and truly believed in me. For that I am so grateful.

Thank you to my siblings. Your consistent support, love and time for me throughout my eczema journey and in creating this book is valued more than you could know. How lucky I am to call my siblings my best friends.

Thank you Baz, for being my best friend since the age of 15 and the man by my side in creating this book. I am so grateful for your calming vibes, your loving support, caring heart and daily advice, especially on the days I have found it difficult sharing my story. You are loved and valued beyond measure.

Finally, thank you to YOU, yes YOU, the wonderful person who has been called to read this book. I deeply appreciate you and wish you well for the future! x

Let's Stay In Touch

You can connect with me here. You'll find more eczema resources on my website and on my social channels too!

 thebeautyofeczema.com/Instagram

 thebeautyofeczema.com/Facebook

 thebeautyofeczema.com/Twitter

 thebeautyofeczema.com/YouTube

 thebeautyofeczema.com

#thebeautyofeczema

I'd love to hear from you!

Camille x

36503979R00153

Printed in Great Britain
by Amazon